CHILDCARE TOP TIPS

Top 10 Tips From 24 Industry Experts To Transform Your Business

By Nick Williams and 23 other industry experts

Child Care Top Tips

Web: www.childcaretoptips.com

Email: support@childcarebusinessgrowth.com

Contents

Acknowledgements

To all our amazing coaches, consultants and business owners who made this book possible. You are all experts in your field, and we are extremely honored to have you contribute to this book and share your knowledge with the child care community.

Brian Duprey

Cris Rodriguez

Sindye Alexander

Dennis Yu

Shana Isaac

Kimberley Taylor

Andrew Lock

Jenna Williams

Joy Maxwell

Summer Picha

Martin Bing

Debbie Lawson

Samantha Phillips

Lauren Lavington

Vanessa Dooley

Beth Cannon

Asia Rivers

Nekea Whitson

Ben McAdam

Kathe O'Dea Petchel

Daphene Booker-Harris

Vernon Mason Jr

Jessica Johnsen

And a special thanks to all the team at Childcare Business Growth. Without you, none of this would be possible. Thank you for all your hard work and everything you do to help our clients succeed.

Introduction

Hey, thanks for taking the time to read this book. We know your time is precious, so I'll get stuck right in. You see, I love books and absorbing more information, but the problem is, you often end up buying a particular book on a topic that usually has more information that you need, and you often need to spend lots of time finding the exact content that you're looking for. So, the reason why I wanted to publish this book was because I had an idea - What if we could pull together some of the top industry experts and ask them to give us their top 10 bullet points on their specialism without any 'fluff'.

So, that's exactly what we did. We've broken the book down into the following sections:

Vision and Mindset

Time Management

The **5 Core Areas** of running a business - **Marketing**, **Sales**, **Operations**, **Delivery** and **Finance**

And finally, we move on to **Scale**.

Success leaves clues, and most successful entrepreneurs didn't build something from scratch. They looked at what was working for others and then tweaked it to their own model.

Well, that's my goal for you with this book. Rather than search for a needle in a haystack; whenever you're having a challenge, or looking for some advice on a particular topic, I want you to be able to pick up this book and go right to the answer.

Please remember that each author / industry expert is expressing their own opinions and not the opinions of other authors within the book. Yes, you may even find some experts talk about the same or similar topic, but their advice will be different. That's totally fine. The book is here to give you that advice from multiple sources and allow you to make the right decision for you and your business.

I hope you enjoy the book and get the answers you're searching for...

VISION AND MINDSET

Defining your Vision, Mission and Culture for your Business

Nick Williams

In this chapter, we are going to be looking at everything that defines the core of your business and why it's so important to have these things in place as early as possible!

From your vision and values, right through to your customer service and golden rules, it's important to keep reviewing these regularly.

When I first started in business I paid no attention to any of this, and I honestly thought it was just nonsense. However, I quickly came to realize that putting all these steps in place is vitally important when it comes to shaping the future success of your business.

I learned the hard way and hired people that didn't have the same beliefs or values as the company, and this impacted not only team morale but also customer service too. So, don't just skip over this chapter because you'll likely pay the price in the long run...

1. Defining Your Vision

So, what is a vision? To begin creating your vision you need to establish and define the most important things that you want your business to achieve.

It's time to ask yourself some questions that will help you determine your vision:

What will your business look like?

Who will it serve? Is there a particular type of customer?

What hours will you be open?

What problem do you solve for others?

And what makes you stand out?

Having a clear vision will give you direction and help you stay guided on your journey towards that vision.

Take the time to answer the questions above and create a clear vision for your business.

2. Identifying Your Values

Your values are the core beliefs and guiding principles that govern everything that you do within your business. They help differentiate you from your competition, and they communicate what's important to you. They shape your culture, attract your ideal customers and most importantly, come from the heart!

Without clear core values, you leave yourself in a place of uncertainty...

Here are some examples of core values of well-known brands that I'm sure you recognize. Let's just take the time to run through them.

Build-A-Bear	Virgin Airlines	Facebook
Reach	We think customer	Focus on Impact
Learn	We lead the way	Move fast
Di-bear-sity	We do the right thing	Be bold
Colla-bear-ate	We are determined to deliver	Be open
Give	Together we make a difference	Build social value
Cele-bear-ate		

I'm sure you already relate to a few of these core values! Plus, if you looked at this same list without the company names being visible, you could probably still successfully identify who these companies are. So it's really important to make sure your core values form the foundation of everything you do.

If you don't already have core values written down, take the time to come up with at least four core values that will form the basis of your company's beliefs and outline everything you want to achieve within your business. These will be your guiding principles.

We've created a list of over 500 core values that you can choose from. To access this free download, go to www.childcaretoptips.com/resources

3. Understanding Your Mission Statement

Here's a great example of a childcare provider that has clearly defined their company values and understands the importance of this for the success of their business:

"Our vision, positive, caring relationships based on trust and respect, are at the heart of our philosophy. We have a clear vision of what we want to achieve at Kings Wellies Nursery, to provide a safe, happy, caring, secure and stimulating environment for your child. To enable all children to develop their capabilities as successful learners, confident individuals, responsible citizens, and effective contributors to society. To help all children to prepare for the future. King Wellies Nursery, is a place to learn, develop, and grow happy, healthy children."

What I love about this is that they have articulated the core of their business into a clear message that not only attracts the families that they want to serve, but it helps them attract the right staff that have the same values and beliefs as the owners. Having a similar statement for your business ensures that you will be able to do the same.

4. What's Your Why?

Once you know your Vision, it's really important that next, you understand your *why*. There's a famous talk available online by a gentleman called Simon Sinek. It is a TEDtalk that explores the importance of your *why*.

Here is a quick summary of his talk:

Most businesses understand what they do. They understand how they do it, but they don't understand the reason *why*. It's really important to understand what you do (which is providing great quality childcare services), how you do that, how do you offer those services, what hours you provide care, and what type of program you follow. But most importantly, why are you doing this? What is the impact that you are going to make? This is where every other foundational principle comes from. It's really understanding your "why".

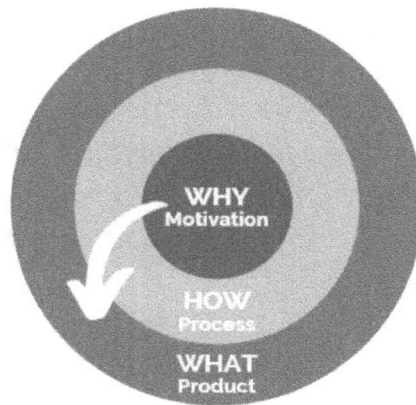

Here are some examples of what may drive you in your business:

To unlock the potential of every child

To achieve your own business goals

To provide outstanding care for children

To be your own boss and deliver care the way you think it should be done

Because you want to be at home with your children, whilst also working.

These are just a few examples. The challenge is for you to come up with at least two reasons why you want to run your own childcare business, because when you have those tough days, which you will, you'll need to remind yourself exactly why you're doing this!

5. Creating Your Vision

Here are four steps to creating your Vision:

- Starting with your core values, paint a picture in your mind of a better future
- A powerful vision is about more than just money or business growth
- It is about making life better for others

- Dream big and bold! Even if only partially achieved you'll get greater results than a wimpy vision fully achieved.

Here's an example of a company vision statement:

To provide outstanding childcare in a home-from-home environment where all children feel happy and settled in. By providing an enabling environment for children to explore, learn, and develop, and forming great relationships with all of my families. So that I can become the most sought-after childcare provider in my area.

Take the time to personalize your why statement to you, and it will not only help you attract the families that have the same beliefs as you, but it will also help you attract the right team members too.

6. Maintaining Quality Standards

I'm a huge Disney fan in terms of the way they run their business. I'm fascinated by the way they can get thousands of employees to take ownership of their decisions without having to rely on a senior team member to guide them all the time. They do this by creating and prioritizing quality standards.

Here's how Disney prioritize their quality standards.

Courtesy _____	Safety _____
Courtesy involves knowing the needs, wants and emotions of each person. Courteous Cast Members... • treat every guest as a VIP • know the answers to questions (or find them) • give the personal touch • treat other cast members with courtest • smile • use friendly phrases • are assertively friendly	Safety provides for the welfare of the Guests and Cast Members through the use of the following... • design considerations • environmental protection • emergency services • prevention • policy and procedures • security • training
Efficiency _____	**Show _____**
Efficiency involves providing for smooth operation through a combination of facilities, systems and Cast Members in regard to... • capacity of facility • guest flow patterns • operational readiness • sales • speed of service • space utilisation	Show creates a seamless Guest Experience through the use of the following... • Cast Member appearance • Cast Members as performers as well as providers of service • costumes and documentation • good show/bad show approach • show quality review • standard manuals • theming

We've recorded a video on how companies prioritize these quality standards. To access this free resource, go to www.childcaretoptips.com/resources

What would your quality standards be in your childcare business?

7. Establish Your Culture

Setting your culture right from the start will ensure the business grows the way you want it to grow. Think about the following when creating your company culture:

How will you communicate with your parents?

What will a typical day look like?

How do you celebrate and reward - children, families, and of course your staff?

How will you encourage the children?

It's all well and good you setting up your business now, but if you want to grow and expand your business to maybe take on more team members, you want to ensure you have these things dialed in right from the start.

Here's the culture and ethos for our business:

STAY LIGHT, MOVE FAST - Implement the things that move the dial the most.

DON'T OUTSOURCE YOUR THINKING - We want solutions over problems.

FORGIVENESS RATHER THAN PERMISSION - Empowered to 'do' without waiting for instructions or consent.

TEAM OF EXPERTS WHO FIGHT FOR EACH OTHER - We are experts in our field and always have each other's back.

SEED THE VISION - Always looking to improve, grow, succeed & motivate.

8. Creating Your Manifesto

I first heard about this concept from a company called Lady Boss. What I love about a manifesto is that it gives everyone a cause and a purpose to stand behind and feel a part of.

Be sure to look up the Lady Boss manifesto and you'll see exactly how they've inspired thousands of women all around the World.

We also have a manifesto here at Childcare Business Growth:

I PROVIDE Great Childcare

I SHAPE Future Generations

I STAND OUT From The Competition

I CREATE My Destiny

I NEVER Give Up

I STAY Focussed

I GIVE No Excuses

You can see how this is relatable to a child care professional. Do you have a manifesto in your business? If not, it's definitely worth the time putting one in place.

9. The Quality Service Model

People don't just buy things, they buy expectations about the quality of performance and service they will receive.

Price, quality, and features are not enough to ensure repeat business for most businesses, and just because a parent has chosen your setting, doesn't mean they won't change their minds and go elsewhere.

There are 5 key aspects of quality service:

Customer Experience - the operating priorities that ensure a quality customer experience.

Environment - the setting, what does it look and feel like.

Staff - the employees responsible for delivering the care.

Process - the systems and operations that help to deliver the outstanding service.

Integration - alignment of all systems, software and delivery to ensure a seamless customer experience.

So, take the time to rate your business against these five areas (1 being the highest and five being the lowest) and identify what you can do to improve these areas.

10. Your Mission Statement

Your mission statement spells out your objective as a company to your staff, managers, target audience, customers and job applicants. You should be specific and concise, use simple words, and avoid jargon and acronyms.

The statement is not a tagline or slogan, it also is not your business vision - the mission statement's purpose is to *communicate*.

What's the difference between a Mission Statement and a Brand Promise?

Mission Statement: To describe what your company does from an internal perspective. To inspire and motivate your team.

Brand Promise: Externally focussed. Crafted to hold your business accountable for delivering a consistent customer experience.

Below is a 4-step process to creating your Mission Statement:

4 step process

It needs to be:
✓ Clear   ✓ Concise   ✓ Short   ✓ Concrete

Always start with a "to verb"

We exist to ....

Our mission is to ....

Name your target

Who are you trying to reach?   Families

Our mission is to help families....

End with your outcome

.... by providing high quality childcare and exceptional customer service

Our mission is to help families by providing high quality childcare and exceptional customer

In summary, your vision, values and culture provide the foundation of your entire child care business. They should be the one thing you consider within all aspects of your role. Question yourself and observe your team when carrying out daily duties, from setting up the room to carrying out activities with the children, to see whether the practice is a reflection of what you set out to achieve. You should always share your vision, values, and culture with your families, so they know what to expect from you.

Ten Core Mindset Habits of Successful

Child Care Business Owners - Brian & Carol Duprey

It is impossible to succeed in a child care business without the proper mindset. Your mindset needs to be right for your skillset to help you achieve your goals.

Building your business without the proper mindset is like trying to run a marathon wearing a 100-pound weight belt. You may eventually get to the end, but it will take you ten times as long and you will be completely worn out when you get there.

We have compiled these ten core mindset habits and if you do all ten each and every day, you will achieve your child care goals much faster, be a much happier person, and truly enjoy the journey.

1. Listen to a Positive Podcast or Audiobook While Commuting

Your daily commute should be an educational commute. You are a busy person and need to compound your time as much as possible. Listening to the news or music may seem like a great distraction, but this is valuable time that can be used to help your business grow.

Make a list of five positive podcasts or a favorite positive audiobook you enjoy and each day on the way to or from work play that day's episode. On Monday morning be sure to play **The Child Care Millionaire Podcast** to set up your week! If you have not yet subscribed, you can find it on your favorite podcast player.

Have four other podcasts you enjoy or an audiobook that is positive so when you arrive at work you have already put positivity into your brain and you are ready for action.

Starting the day with positive energy helps to release chemicals in the brain to automatically put you in a better mood. You will be able to react to stressors at work better, be nicer to people, and feel better as well. Your employees will notice the difference in how you are acting at work, a more positive person for sure!

2. Look at Your Dreams and Goals Daily

There is power in visioning, which is closing your eyes and seeing yourself in possession of your dreams and goals. Every successful athlete uses this technique before the competition to see themselves as victorious. We can attest that this works as we have used this most of our adult life.

You need to write down all of your short and long-term business and personal goals. Make sure they are SMART goals.

Specific - Must be as clear as possible, no ambiguity.

Measurable - Something you can quantify and measure results.

Attainable - Something that you would be able to attain with reasonable effort.

Realistic - You must be able to accomplish this goal realistically.

Timely - Must have a timeline for completion.

Also, be sure to list 100 dreams that you wish to accomplish in your lifetime. Want to jump out of an airplane? Climb Mount Everest? Run the Boston Marathon? These are dreams. Goals would be a dream with a deadline. I will climb Mount Everest in July of 2025 and here is my plan to prepare. A goal is a dream with a plan and a timeline.

One way to track your business and personal goals and dreams is with our ***Child Care Mindset Dreams, Goals, and Gratitude Journal***. If you have not done so you can order it on our website at ChildCareMillionaire.com/Books

Once you have all of your dreams and goals written, you need to look at them daily. By looking at them daily your brain will put forth action to help you achieve them, oftentimes without conscious thought. Your brain is a powerful tool, and teasing it with your goals and dreams will put it in high gear to make them happen for you!

3. Laugh Daily

There are incredible health benefits to laughing. Laughing releases endorphins, the body's feel-good chemical. Endorphins promote an overall sense of well-being and can even temporarily relieve pain. Laughter also protects the heart and can help you live longer. Laughter also releases serotonin which is the chemical used in anti-depressants.

One thing we do to make sure we laugh each and every day is to record some funny sitcoms on our DVR and each night before we go to bed we watch 20 minutes of a funny sitcom. (Our recordings include Seinfeld/Two and a Half Men/King of Queens/Last Man Standing/Impractical Jokers). Find what makes you laugh and spend the last part of each day, releasing endorphins into your bloodstream. You will sleep better, feel better, live longer, be happier and wake up the next day ready to take on the world.

If television is not your thing, you can watch a YouTube funny clip as well. Just be sure to use blue-blocking glasses if you are on your phone within an hour of bedtime. The blue light of your phone can disrupt sleep patterns. (Some phones will auto-adjust the light in the evening to protect you).

As the old saying goes, laughter is the best medicine, and now you know it is true. Go make a plan to change your life by adding laughter to your daily routine, you will thank us for it.

4. Meditate for Five Minutes or More per Day

The faster the pace you have in your daily routine, the more you need to slow down and meditation is the ultimate form of slowing down. It amounts to nothing more than sitting still with completely empty thoughts for a period of time.

We are busy people. Brian hates sleep and thinks it is unproductive. Carol can sleep 12 hours a night. We are truly opposites. While we are awake though we are going at 100 miles per hour from the time we wake up until the time we go to bed.

Stopping to meditate is harder for Brian because at first, he thought it was super unproductive. Why would anyone want to waste time sitting on the floor in a dark room, seems silly he would say.

At first, it will seem awkward. Actually, it will seem that way for a while, until you start feeling the benefits of relaxation. The good news is that there are free apps and websites that will help you meditate and stay focused on doing nothing.

A simple way to do this is to sit on the floor in a quiet room with no cell phone, no smartwatch, and some relaxing music (no words) playing in the background. Close your eyes and concentrate on your breathing. Breathe deeply in through your nose and out slowly of your mouth. Find a happy place you can go to that requires no active thought.

We both go to a beach as our happy place. We imagine we are sitting in the sand watching the sunset in the Caribbean. We picture that in our minds and just watch the ocean waves. Whenever thoughts creep in our minds, we re-center and go back to the ocean. We do this as long as we can. At first, we could only do a few minutes, eventually, we built it up to 10 minutes and sometimes more. It's not how long you do it, just the act of slowing down even for a few minutes will really help to re-center you and make you more productive when you do get back to work.

5. Write in a Gratitude Journal Daily

The faster the pace you have in your daily routine, the more you need to slow down and be thankful for what you have. One way to do this is by having a gratitude journal. If you have not already purchased your **Child Care Millionaire Goals, Dreams, and Gratitude Journal** now would be a good time to do so by going to ChildCareMillionaire.com/Books.

Each day write 1-3 things you are thankful for in your life. There are spaces in our journal for over 1,000 gratitudes, so you will have plenty of room to write them out.

You may be asking what the purpose is of writing out what you are grateful for. The reason you do this is twofold.

1. It helps you to really focus on the important things in life you are thankful for.

2. When you are sad, lonely, or depressed you can pull out your journal and see how truly blessed you actually are.

Set a reminder in your phone to tell you to write in your journal at a specific time each day, or find a time that works for you. Some ideas on what time to do it are:

1. Right when you wake up daily.

2. Before bed.

3. After workout.

4. While waiting for your coffee to brew.

5. During breakfast or lunch.

6. Before or after meditation.

Whatever time you decide to utilize be consistent in going to your goals, dreams, and gratitude journal. Doing so will completely change your life, making you a positive person that everyone enjoys being around. You will feel better, be much happier, learn to enjoy life, and be a much better boss, husband, wife, mother, father, and human. We are grateful you are taking the next step to a better you!

6. Practice One Random Act of Kindness a Day

We live in a selfish world. Everyone is so darn busy that we tend to put ourselves in a bubble and forget we are a small piece of humanity. We forget that our lives are interdependent on other people each and every day.

When you give someone a gift have you ever felt happier than the person receiving it? It feels so good to do something nice for someone else doesn't it? When you hand your employee a bonus do you feel proud of yourself? Unfortunately, many people do nice things for others and expect the other person to do a nice thing for them in return. You give them a gift assuming they will turn around and give you one. Buy a friend's lunch and expect him to buy it the next time.

How about buying a stranger's lunch? How about paying the toll for the car behind you? How about paying for a stranger's groceries at the supermarket? How about paying the tuition for a parent at your school who is struggling? How about putting a bag of groceries on your elderly neighbor's porch?

You may be saying I cannot afford to help someone else financially. How about holding the door for several people at the bank? How about mowing the neighbor's yard or shoveling their driveway? How about sending an email to someone and letting them know how much you appreciate them?

By practicing one random act of kindness a day you trigger the feel-good chemical dopamine in the brain. It feels really good to help someone else out, especially if it is done randomly and preferably without them knowing it is you. By them not knowing you were the one, it feels more genuine and not coming from a place of reciprocity where you are expecting something in return.

One thing we do is pray about who to help. God, please put people in our path that need us to bless them. It always tends to work out that the people we help were the ones that needed the most help.

Go try this and let us know how it feels. It may seem weird at first, but watch the reaction when people are blessed by a stranger. There is no better feeling than lifting someone else up.

7. Smile in the Mirror Twice a Day

Loving yourself is hard for most people, but it is necessary to have a great business mindset. Looking at yourself in the mirror is a very hard thing to do for a lot of people, as many people are not happy with what they see.

Take a stickie and write the word SMILE on it and put it right in the middle of your mirror. When you brush your teeth in the morning and the evening, smile at yourself. Look deeply into your own eyes and show those pearly whites.

Smiling will cause your brain to start thinking of yourself positively. Since the brain is a computer, whatever you program in (negative or positive) is what comes out. Most people think negative thoughts when you look in the mirror, by smiling at yourself you trigger happy thoughts of yourself and your brain will react by making you happier and giving you more confidence in your appearance.

Please go write the SMILE note now and put it on your mirror, if you do not do it right now you will probably forget. Procrastination is the key to failure and you are a winner. Please go do it now, we will wait right here for you while you take care of this.

Did you do it? Or did you say I will do it later? Those who succeed in business take action and do not put off success habits. If you are reading this you want to improve your life, trust us that this will help you. Go do it now if you have not done it.

Congratulations! This is the start of a beautiful friendship (with yourself). You are the most important person in your life, without you, there would be no you. Yes, that sounds dumb, but it's true. A happier you will be a much better person to everyone around you, especially yourself. Go enjoy the newer, happier you. SMILE!!!

8. Read Ten Pages a Day in a Positive Mental Attitude Book (PMA)

If you are a business owner or a director you are a busy person and may think you do not have time to read. Reading a PMA book is stimulating your brain with successful thoughts that will manifest in action for the rest of your life.

A Positive Mental Attitude is a philosophy that having an optimistic outlook attracts a positive outcome in life.

Ten pages take the average person 10-15 minutes to read. If you cannot find 15 minutes a day to make yourself a better person, you need to shift your time priorities. I can promise you that have the time, you just have to find it. What can you do differently in your current daily routine to find the time to make yourself a better person?

Early in our business-building career, we started reading PMA books right before bed, and our brains would think about that positive all night long. The next day when we awoke our brains would work to make those positive thoughts a reality without us actively thinking about them. We became successful by reading about success and modeling what we were reading in our daily routine.

The average CEO in America reads one new book a week. It's no wonder that the average salary of a CEO is 475 times greater than the people who are employed at the company. Do you think they started reading when they became a CEO? NO! Reading about success turned them into a success!

You are a computer programmer. Bet you never thought of yourself as one. You get to program your brain each and every day of your life. You can program it with trash, or you can program it with a PMA book and have lifetime access to successful strategies that will benefit you financially for life. Fifteen minutes a day can make you millions of dollars over your lifetime. Can you find the time now?

9. Practice Positive Self-Talk

This is one of the hardest things we will ask you to do. Right now we would like you to pull out your phone and open your camera and point it at yourself. Repeat after us: I AM AWESOME.

Now we know you probably did not do it, so let's try again and this time YELL IT!

I AM AWESOME!!!!!

It was hard saying that, wasn't it? Why? Because most people have a negative self-image. Most people do not think they are awesome, they think of themselves negatively.

The human brain cannot tell the difference between the truth and a lie. If you tell your brain negative thoughts about yourself, it will believe it and make sure it manifests itself. If you feed your brain positive thoughts, it will manifest positivity and attract positive people to you.

I FEEL GREAT!

I say that all the time. Find what phrase works for you. Something that will make you feel better and give yourself a jolt of positivity when you need it the most.

Some people like to have an affirmation list that they read several times a day. Here is an example of an affirmation list.

I FEEL GREAT

I AM AWESOME

I AM A LEAN MEAN POSITIVITY MACHINE

PEOPLE LOVE ME

I LOVE ME

I AM AN AMAZING PERSON

PEOPLE WANT TO HANG AROUND ME

I AM PERFECT JUST THE WAY I AM

Find what works for you and place them on your bathroom mirror and repeat them out loud while smiling. If you do this twice a day, your life will change beyond anything you have ever done in your life. You will feel so good about yourself, will begin acting differently, and will be happy with where you are in life.

WARNING: Negative people will be repulsed by you and will try to bring you down to their level. Negative people cannot stand positive people, so you may need to go find some positive friends to hang around with. The good news is they are much more fun to be around!

10. The Past is the Past, it's Time to Live in the NOW!

Many of you reading this are being held back by a traumatic past. There is something that happened to you that you cannot move forward from. Imagine a swimmer trying to swim with an anchor tied around their neck, this is what it is like trying to get through life while living in the past.

There is so much power in living in the now. It is such a gift that it was named the "present". It is the only parcel of time we have any control over. So many people are stuck in the past (depressed) or worried about the future (anxiety) and are not living for today, for the now. There is incredible power in focusing on the here and now and knowing that this is the one area of your life you have complete control over and you can shape it and mold it into anything you wish!

You cannot change the past, it happened. So many people have had unthinkable things happen to them, and have been able to move past it while others have been stuck and not been able to move forward. Many people have turned to drugs or alcohol to mask the pain of the past, only to make their present miserable and ruin their future.

We highly recommend starting with these 10 Core Mindset Habits to start changing your life for the better. All of these habits are happening in the present. We also recommend reading the book ***The Happiness Guide for Early Childhood Educators: Secrets to Living Your Best Life in and out of the Classroom***. This is a life-changing book! It will cause you to think differently about life, which will help you to make better decisions.

If this does not help, please get professional help. There is no shame in getting help to move past trauma. Once you are able to move past the past you will be able to remove that anchor and live a life in the present that is truly a gift.

Every day is made up of thousands of now moments. The future is always the future, it never comes. The past will always be the past, whether it was 5 minutes ago or 5 years ago. You can't change either. There is only now and more now. It's the only part of life you have any control over. Each minute you get a new minute of now to live in. So enjoy living in the moment. It's a wonderful life if you take the time to enjoy the gift of the present.

Brian & Carol Duprey are best-selling authors, certified child care coaches, motivational speakers, and hosts of The Child Care Millionaire Podcast. Follow them @briancarolduprey on Instagram, @CCMCouple on Facebook, and at www.ChildCareGenius.com.

know exactly what is expected and are provided with the training, equipment, or supplies to fulfill those expectations.

You can create a system for any repeatable processes in your business, such as how to run an invoice, create a lunch menu, request a day off, open or close a classroom, inspect a playground, turn in lesson plans, report an injury, or organize an event. Creating systems isn't complicated, it is simply your method of doing something so that it can be done the same way, over and over, as efficiently as possible by any person on your team.

With systems in place, leaders can focus on bigger picture things rather than being bogged down in day-to-day operations. When leaders are able to be the true visionary of their company, they can lead their teams forward to places of growth and excellence that would otherwise not be possible.

3. Hire the RIGHT Team

If you've been working on creating a positive culture in your child care program, you want to be sure you hire quality team members that will contribute to your efforts and blend in well with the other stellar staff members already on the team.

It's a good idea to create an avatar of your ideal employee, so you know exactly who you are looking for. Write down all of the qualities you find desirable in a staff member, and describe the behaviors you think they'd exhibit. Knowing this will help you quickly identify the top candidates when you are interviewing, which is crucial because bringing the wrong person onto the team can quickly disrupt the happy culture you've worked so hard to create.

In his book, *Traction*, Gino Wickman calls this concept RPRS, or making sure you have the Right Person in the Right Seat. Having the *right person* refers to hiring someone who aligns with your values and mission. Putting that person into the right seat, or correct position, involves matching their qualifications and skills to the position you need to fill.

Of the two, *right person* is usually the most important aspect to consider when hiring for a child care role. If you employ someone that has a positive attitude, wants to make a difference, and aligns with your company values, but is inexperienced in early education, you can usually train them on the skills they need.

In the same way that you need to be careful with who you ADD to your team, you need to be careful with who you KEEP on your team. When you have a poor performer or a negative Nellie on your team, it's important to get to the bottom of it and correct the issue as soon as possible, or risk the spread of negativity in your workplace culture. Have a private heart-to-heart meeting with the person in question to see if there are any issues that can be resolved or improvements made. But if you cannot see a way to keep this person on your team, let them go as quickly as possible. You may need some time to find their replacement, but begin the process quickly. Keeping toxic team members on your team for too long will discourage your top-notch teachers and make them want to look for greener pastures.

4. Design an Outstanding Onboarding and Training Plan

It only takes seven seconds to make a first impression. How do you think your new hire will feel if they arrive for their first day of work and aren't sure where to park or what to wear? Do you think they will feel welcomed or valued if they are greeted by a receptionist who isn't aware that they are expected to begin work that day? Absolutely not. They will begin questioning whether they made the right decision to accept this job while they wait for you and your team to get their act together.

It is so important to make a great first impression when you finally do make a great hire! Be sure to go out of your way to do everything possible to make their onboarding experience outstanding. From the moment they arrive, you want them to feel like they just accepted the best job in the world! Be prepared and add special little touches to let them know you are excited about adding them to the team. This can include getting them flowers or taking them to lunch to welcome them, taking their picture for the staff wall, or having their locker labeled ahead of time. It doesn't have to cost a lot. Just find some unique ways to let them know that they matter to you and your business from day one!

In addition to adding a few wow factors into your onboarding process, you also need to consider your training process. Every new employee needs to go through training, no matter how much experience or education they have. They will need to learn how to deliver your service according to your brand standards. Burger King, McDonalds, and Wendy's all serve hamburgers. If a former Wendy's employee begins working at McDonalds, but does not change his system for building a hamburger, it would create a huge problem. So, set your teachers and caregivers up for success by providing proper training, so they have the tools they need to be successful in their roles.

To accomplish this, think about everything they need to know to deliver the high-quality service you expect, and create a training program that will truly give them the answers and tools they need. If you get your onboarding and training process right, your new employees will be excited to be a part of your amazing school and work hard to perpetuate the great culture and high standards that you've established.

5. Take Care of Your Employees

As much as your staff love to work with children and to make a difference, they are likely working because they need a job to pay their bills. Be sure you are valuing your employees by paying them the highest wage that you can. I am not suggesting that you overextend your budget, just that you are not stingy when creating your pay scale and center budget.

In addition to wages, create a benefits or perks package that will appeal to your staff. Sometimes, because budgets are tight, owners think they "can't afford" to offer a bunch of perks to their employees. While you might not be able to afford extremely expensive benefits such as health insurance, there ARE lots of things you CAN offer.

Here are a few ideas of things you could add to your "Benefits/Perks" package. It's possible that you're already doing some of these things, but you aren't highlighting them as "Employee Benefits." Sometimes all it takes is re-framing and emphasizing all the good things that you offer your staff in a nice little flyer. Also, if you can put a monetary value to these benefits, it may also make a difference in how their wages/benefits are perceived. When you highlight the positive, your staff can see it more clearly and feel more valued.

- Life Insurance

- Aflac or other Supplemental Insurance

- Child Care Discount

- Paid Training Hours

- Continuing Education Support (T.E.A.C.H Scholarship)

- Breakroom Stocked with Snacks and/or Special Staff Lunches

- Meals Provided

- A Budget for Classroom Supplies

- Paid Planning Time out of the Classroom

- Direct Deposit

- Weekly or Bi-Weekly Pay Schedule

- Either a Flexible Schedule or Regular Schedule

- PTO, Vacation Time, Paid Holidays

- Birthday Celebration/Reward

- Career Ladder/Pay Scale

- Performance Bonuses

- Staff Awards/Recognition

- Help with Transportation or Gas

- Gym or Fitness Membership

- Staff Retreats or Activities

You may have other things that you do to take care of your employees. Whatever you offer them, be sure to include it in your employee benefit list and begin promoting your huge package of perks. Highlighting all of the great things you do for staff in a well-thought-out Employee Perks or Benefit Package will help you attract and keep the best staff, and the best staff contribute to an awesome company culture!

6. Build Relationships

Employees that have a good relationship with their bosses are more engaged and effective in their work and stay with the company longer. This is why actively working to build relationships with your employees is so important.

Just like with any successful relationship, you must continually work at it. People are not robots. Your staff members need to FEEL like you care about them, or they will be less likely to care very much about you or the work they do for your company.

In any human relationship, whether a professional working relationship or an intimate personal relationship, there must be an emotional element. If feelings of connection and care are absent between the two parties, the relationship will die. The same is true if there is an overarching sense of resentment or hostility.

Find ways to build relationships with your employees! Nobody likes to feel like they are just a number. People naturally seek connections and commonalities with other people. They want to feel like they belong. Prioritize taking an interest in your staff members on a personal level.

Genuinely show interest with each person you add to your team by making deliberate efforts to get to know them. Ask questions, learn about their interests, and celebrate with them when they accomplish a goal. How did the dance recital go? Where is their son's basketball game next week? Are they team Star Wars or Star Trek? Do you enjoy the same hobbies or sports? Find ways to make connections. When leaders look for ways to make employee relationships about more than work and purposefully look for ways to connect, it will impact staff retention rates, workplace happiness, and foster a sense of belonging.

7. Prioritize Quality and Professionalism

Don't cut corners or ignore licensing rules unless the inspector is on-site. Instead, work to build a quality early learning environment with the highest standards. Become the center of choice in your area, and your team will feel like they are a part of a quality organization and have pride in their job.

Encourage professionalism by providing professional development opportunities over and above the minimum requirements. When you can find ways to invest in your team by providing professional development opportunities, it can improve your workplace culture because it sends a message to your team that you value them and are willing to invest in their growth.

You can provide additional training in the form of online classes, local or state conferences, bringing guest speakers into your school, tuition assistance, or enrolling them in a CDA program.

8. Trust and Empower Your Team

You must believe in your team and trust them to do their job well. You hired them for a reason. You liked them, they impressed you, and they showed promise. Now, give them a chance to do well! Too many child care owners or directors hold onto the reins (of tasks that could be delegated) much too tightly because they are afraid that "IT" won't get done "RIGHT."

If you spend all your time micromanaging everything that your team does, you are defeating the purpose of having a team. You are not freeing up your own time to focus on bigger picture, visionary things - so you're staying stuck. Additionally, you are denying your team members the chance to take on more responsibility and keeping them stuck in menial roles. Whether you mean to or not, doing this just demonstrates to them that you don't trust them, or don't think they are "good enough," both of which are morale killers.

Empower team members by giving them extra areas of responsibility and honor them with a title. You can create new roles or positions such as committee leaders, resident experts, or project managers to share some of the load and give talented and willing members of your team opportunities to shine.

Having a strong positive belief in your team and demonstrating your trust in their abilities is essential to a positive workplace culture.

9. Show Recognition & Appreciation

When people feel appreciated, they will go above and beyond for you. They will also likely be more willing to be flexible and adapt when there are occasional bumps in the road. They will feel like a valued part of your organization and see themselves as part of the solution. However, when staff feel forgotten and taken for granted, their negative energy can start to ooze out into the atmosphere (even unintentionally), infecting the center environment.

Be on the lookout for the "caught being good" moments among your employees, and then find ways to publicly recognize and reward them for their great work. There are many ways to do this, but try to get creative. It can be just a quick word of praise said in front of the other teachers in the classroom, a shout-out on social media, a handwritten thank-you note, a mention at a staff meeting, a certificate of appreciation, a small gift of thanks, extra "points" or "org bucks" awarded, and more.

The most important thing is that the employee knows that you noticed their hard work and that you appreciate their efforts. When you are able to recognize positive behaviors and contributions in a meaningful way, it builds relationships and contributes to higher job satisfaction. Employees that are happy in their work will help keep the work environment happy as well.

10. Facilitate Fun & Friendships

Make it a point to bring fun into the workplace. I am not talking about just fun for the kiddos, but fun for the staff! This will go a long way to improving your workplace culture. Being in the child care business, it's almost like a license to have fun. We are not stuck in stuffy offices or required to wear suits, ties, or pantyhose. We play with play-doh, build with blocks, and make wacky animal noises for a living. We work in the perfect environment to get silly, so as leaders, look for intentional ways to make work FUN for your team.

Have silly costume contest days, create a fun break room where your team can relax on their break, surprise them with yummy snacks, organize pot luck lunches, decorate their door or locker on their birthday, do impromptu trivia about licensing or policies and give prizes, have a local food truck deliver lunch for the team, create secret handshakes, declare random dance-offs. The sky is the limit, but get creative and find ways to bring fun INTO the workplace whenever possible.

Also, did you know that when an employee feels like they have a "best friend" at work they are more engaged, more productive, and LESS LIKELY to quit? Do all you can to facilitate fun and friendships between staff in your child care center and you are sure to create a culture that your team will want to remain a part of for years to come.

** To learn more or dive deeper into creating and maintaining a positive workplace culture, find Sindye's book on Amazon: *Relationship Roadmap: Real-World Strategies for Building a Positive, Collaborative Culture in Your Preschool.*

****

Sindye Alexander

Sindye Alexander has over 25 years of experience in the child care field. She's owned and directed both in-home and commercial child care centers. After working with several business coaches, and with the help of her amazing team, she was able to grow her in-home child care to a small child care center licensed for 32 children, then move to a larger building expanding to 120 children. Sindye was able to fill her new school just three months after relocating due to her proactive marketing tactics.

Experiencing such massive results in growing her business caused Sindye to fall in love with marketing and the business side of child care. She sold her center in 2016 and joined the Child Care Success Company where she served as the Director of Marketing and as a child care training coach for several years.

Sindye is especially passionate about inspiring child care leaders to create a positive workplace culture. Her book: *Relationship Roadmap: Real-World Strategies for Building a Positive, Collaborative Culture in Your Preschool* is dedicated to providing owners and directors with actionable tips and tactics for doing just that.

She now independently serves several private clients with content and digital marketing services, and is available to train or speak on topics related to workplace culture and marketing.

Sindye resides in northern Michigan with her husband, Chad. They have four grown children and three grandchildren. Sindye values time with her family and enjoys traveling - especially cruising! She loves helping other child care business owners and directors grow and succeed. To inquire about having Sindye speak at your upcoming workshop, conference, or other event: email: sindyealexander88@gmail.com. (You can also find her on Facebook and LinkedIn.

TIME MANAGEMENT

7 Figure Productivity Hacks

Cris Rodriguez

Time is a great equalizer. We all only get 24 hours in a day. So how is it that some of us can get so much more done in those same 24 hours?

Since the birth of my son Cruz, I have become obsessed with productivity and efficiency. Why? Because I absolutely love business. And I love being an entrepreneur. And I LOVE what I do! Can you relate?

But I also know that there is no worldly success that can compensate for failure in the home.

And I made a contract with myself that I was going to be a present parent - which meant that I needed to get a lot of work done in a short period of time so I had more time to spend with my son and family.

I also own 4 businesses: A Marketing Agency, A Consulting Firm, A Martial Arts School, and a Commercial Real Estate Investing Company which meant that every minute of every work day needed to be assigned so that I could maximize my efficiency.

Below you will find my top 10 tips that have helped me become a 7 Figure CEO while also being a super present parent and wife.

1 - Proper Daily Habits

Becoming more productive is a skill set that you can work on improving. For some (mainly A type personalities) it seems to feel more natural, for others, more difficult. Regardless, it is a skill set that can be improved on, and it starts with your daily habits.

Habits are simply the small decisions you make and actions you perform every day. We are going to cover some tactical productivity tips that if you implement into your daily habits you can find massive success.

2 – Time Tracking

"What gets measured gets improved." If you want to lose weight, your personal trainer is going to tell you to start measuring your macros and your weight. If you want to save money, you've got to track where every dollar is spent. If you want to get stronger, you've got to track each one of your lifts. With most things in life, we want to be able to make data driven decisions and if you are wanting to gain more productivity, we've got to start with tracking your time, this way we can see where your "time vampires" are and what you can start automating, delegating, or deleting (more on this in a future tip).

This simple exercise of writing down everything you do in your business for a 2 week time period in 30 minute increments can be absolutely eye-opening and game changing to anyone who is looking to create "more time" in their day.

3 – Delegate & Elevate

One of the most powerful exercises that I have ever completed is called the "Delegate and Elevate" worksheet by EOS (Entrepreneurial Operating System).

Once you have completed your Time Tracking, take a sheet of paper and make 4 quadrants. In the top left quadrant write "Love/Great", in the top right quadrant write "Like/Good". In the bottom left quadrant write "Dislike/Good", and in the bottom right quadrant write "Dislike/Not Good".

Take all of the items on your time tracking sheet that have to do with your business and categorize them into one of these 4 quadrants. Categories of what you absolutely love doing and you are great at, what you like and are good at, what you don't like but are good at, and what you dislike and are not good at.

Then start at the bottom right quadrant (Dislike/Not Good). The goal is to either Automate, Delegate, or Delete each of the items in this list. Once completed, then you work your way over to the "Dislike/Good" list. The ultimate goal is to only be working on items in the top two quadrants.

4 – Time Blocking

Time blocking is a time management method that asks you to divide your day into blocks of time. Each block is then dedicated to accomplishing a specific task, or group of tasks, and only those specific tasks. Most people work off an open ended to-do list of items they need to get done as they are able to.

Instead, when utilizing time blocking, you will start each and every day with a rock solid schedule of not only what you are supposed to be working on - but when you are supposed to be working on it.

5 – Book End Your Day – Morning

Most people are not very productive because they are constantly being bombarded with interruptions. There are usually two times a day where interruptions are a minimum and that's right when you wake up and before you go to sleep. We want to take advantage of these time periods. I recommend "Book Ending" both your morning and your evening with strategies that will help you start your day with your best foot forward and strategies that will help you have a great night sleep being completely prepared for the next day. My Morning Ritual includes coffee and reading, 1 on 1 time with my son, and a workout. When I start my morning this way, I have a great chance of having a very productive day.

6 – Book End Your Day – Evening

The same way that you can have a morning ritual, I suggest having an evening ritual as well. My evening ritual includes journaling, time blocking my next day, writing out any lingering items such as tasks or ideas, and research and development. Doing so allows me to clear my mind and ensures a great nights rest.

7 – Hire a Mentor

There is no need to try and reinvent the wheel. The fastest way to success is hiring someone who has already accomplished what you are setting out to accomplish, listening to what they say, and then doing it exactly as they say. I have mentors in all areas of my life (fitness and nutrition, agency business, martial arts business, relationships, and mindset). Your mentor will be able to help you prioritize your daily tasks so that you are spending more time on the most important items.

8 – 90 Day Game plans

Most people set goals at the beginning of the year and make the mistake of never revisiting them. Whether it's a personal goal or a business goal, you must be revisiting them. One of the ways we do this in our companies is with our 90 Day Game plans. Our Annual Goals are broken down quarterly so they are more digestible and easier to achieve. From company kpi's, to projects, to budgeting

- our team and company lives in these 90 day sprints. Being able to break down your annual goals into quarterly goals, then into monthly goals, and then into daily goals is a positive way for you to stay on track to hit those goals.

9 - Kanban Board

The word kanban is Japanese and roughly translated means "card you can see." It has become very popularized in recent years with major software systems utilizing it for project management. I personally am a fan of a physical kanban board that can be seen from my office desk. I use a white board and post-it notes. My personal kanban has 5 sections (you can have more or less). Those sections are written in columns and are: Ideas, Rocks (90 Day Projects), Doing, Assist, Completed. Each section has post-it notes with the topic/strategy I am trying to implement. The goal is to move the post-it note from Idea to Completed in the 90-day time period that was given.

Having this visual representation of where I am at with my projects is a great daily reminder of where my focus needs to go and also serves as motivation to finish these items.

10 - Personal Assistant

The ultimate productivity hack is delegation with observation. One of the absolute best hires I have ever made is a Personal Assistant. Having someone that can assist me with any area in my companies has been a HUGE time saver. The major issue that seems to occur for most entrepreneurs is that they tend to forget that once they delegate, they must observe the person who they delegated the item to so they can provide feedback. Skipping the observation phase is a huge mistake that will cost you a lot of extra time.

****

With 27 years of Martial Arts Experience and 20 years of Teaching Experience, Professor Cris Rodriguez is a 1st Degree Brazilian Jiu Jitsu Black Belt, 3rd Degree TKD Black Belt, and Co-Owns Gracie PAC MMA, a BJJ & MMA School in Tampa, Florida, with her wife Stephanie.

She has been obsessed with Internet Marketing for the past 10 years and is the Founder of Grow Pro Agency, a Digital Marketing Agency for Martial Arts

Academies with over 240 clients. As a Partner in Marketing with Schools, their core focus is to help school owners gain the freedom they want in their business.

She is also the Digital Marketing Consultant for the Martial Arts Industry Association and runs her own Mastermind Program called "The A Team" and Business Event called "7 Figure CEO".

She earned her Elementary Education Degree from the University of South Florida which has helped her to become an expert in Children's Jiu Jitsu Training & Development.

Cris lives in Tampa, Florida with Stephanie and their three sons Darion, Nate, & Cruz.

Author website link:

www.growproagency.com

Outsourcing

Dennis Yu

Suzanne Valdez is in her mid-50's and lives in Las Vegas, where I have a home. Because of a disability, she's limited in the kinds of work she can do. Every Monday she goes to Costco to grab coconut water, rotisserie chicken, and whatever the pets need. I'm gone 60% of the time (hanging out with cool people like Nick Williams). But when I'm back, the place is tidy, the fridge is stocked, and things smell nice.

I don't think I've done laundry for years.

And that's one of many things I don't worry about anymore because I outsource. Anything that can be documented can be outsourced.

A friend of mine runs a factory in Portland that prints socks with YOUR face on them. Super unique gift that always gets a response from clients (maybe a good birthday gift for parents in your childcare center). But the hassle of finding the right picture (from LinkedIn or Facebook), finding the address, configuring the order, entering a credit card-- I just didn't want to do it.

So I found Mary in the Philippines who does this at a few dollars an hour. And because I had a 10 minute screen share tutorial, a dozen other team members know how to order face socks the exact same way. In fact, we created an entire course called the Thank You Machine to list our favorite items on Amazon Prime (sorted by occasion), canned (but clever) messages to use, and so forth.

So now when we get new clients or people buy any of our products, the gift fulfillment is something I'm not personally involved in. And we've extended this to a thousand different tasks, building what we call the Task Library.

I ask my friends, "Honestly, how many hours per day are you doing stuff that is repetitive?" You know how people respond? Typically, 2-3 hours. Imagine the value of your time-- getting back 3 hours per day, compounding for weeks and even years.

Outsourcing is about working on your business, not in your business, as you've heard in the E-Myth. People don't do it because outsourcing is not the same as automation. You can't just buy some piece of software or a machine. You need a process (which you're getting here) and then people to fit into the process.

Think of your childcare business like a machine. There are many components that ideally run smoothly-- until a child gets sick, a parent doesn't pick up their child on time, a staff member quits, and whatnot. When I worked at American Airlines nearly 25 years ago, we called this OSO (Off Schedule Operations)-- a process to deal with flight attendant strikes, rising fuel prices, competitors venturing into one of our hubs, you get the idea.

The SOPs drive your business so that you ideally don't ever need to be there except when you want. Outsourcing, which is this chapter, is about meshing the people and process together to get you out of stuff you don't want to have to do.

Outsourcing, I'm firmly convinced, is the greatest multiplier of your business, whether you have 10 children or 10,000 across 100 locations-- since time is your most valuable and limited asset. Successful childcare business owners know that they can trade money for time, but not the other way around-- unless they themselves are employees in the business.

Here are 10 steps for you to begin to outsource powerfully:

1. First, determine the value of an hour of your time

What's an hour to spend with your children worth? Or how about an incremental hour of sleep? Or maybe another hour to be able to learn from Nick Williams via this book in your hands? Most owners haven't picked a number before. If you haven't, $100 an hour is a good starting point. Anything below this number, we want to outsource.

2. Make a list of these lower value tasks

Typically, people think of common stuff like janitorial and manual labor. But you can even outsource most aspects of your marketing, operations, and administration. Tim Ferriss, the 4-Hour Work week guy takes it to the extreme by even outsourcing his dating. The only thing you can't outsource is your fitness-- if only someone else could work out for you! You can get creative.

3. Ensure you have a SOP for each task

For example, it could be your exact process to follow up on parents who have just had a tour of the facility. Or items to buy in preparation for a child's birthday party. Maybe it's your process to screen, hire and train up more workers. Sites like lifehacker.com even list out these tasks and offer apps to help you "gamify" your life, as if you lived in a giant simulation. My favorite SOPs are for virtual assistants (also called "international workers") who typically do more structured work like low-level marketing, scheduling, website building, etc...

4. Start outsourcing one task to one person

I have maids that come weekly to my homes in Phoenix and in Las Vegas. We have an army of virtual assistants from the Philippines, Pakistan, Ukraine, and all over the world, all working on a 6 level pay scale with underlying certifications to qualify for their position. But originally, I started with just one guy in India who did website stuff for me at $8/hour.

5. Have at least two people who can do each role

Redundancy will cost you a bit more money. But it's worth it when that one key person gets sick, quits, or isn't available. If you're growing fast, this will help you handle scale and peak periods-- perhaps when you need more people for a holiday campaign at your facility or more people to do a particular thing. Even if you have one person who is only part-time doing your computers and IT support 10 hours a week-- still have another person who is a back-up just in case. You'll thank me for this when the inevitable thing goes south at some point.

6. Create your profile on onlinejobs.ph

Once you've demonstrated you can do it yourself or in-house, then find someone to do it in the Philippines. There are 2 million virtual assistants on that site-- the largest in the world. So whatever you're looking for (just like Amazon), you'll find it there. Maybe it's someone to answer questions about facility tours and pricing-- whether by phone (during your office hours) or social media channels. They can work your hours (even if it's the middle of the night for them). And they have nearly any skill-- even high level consultation skills via Zoom. But you have to have a strict screening process to find the right people. Onlinejobs.ph is my favorite place to outsource because the Filipinos are super loyal and happy to fit into processes. We say processes make you money, while projects cost you money.

7. Fill in the gaps with freelancers:

Fiverr and UpWork are my personal favorites. We've hired hundreds from these sites. But we know freelancer.com, turing.com, and toptal.com are great, too-- with each site specializing in a type of worker. Just remember that people fail in hiring because they don't have super clear requirements, don't have a pre-screen process (so we don't interview everyone right off the bat), and because their standards are too low. We typically hire one out of every 200 applicants, which is normal for marketing type roles. Remember that freelancers are for projects-- a clear deliverable with a defined end date, while virtual assistants are for on-going processes.

8. Establish a manager:

Once you get above 3 outsourced workers, the management burden will start to eat away your time from running your childcare center. I like to hire senior people to start, knowing they will be training and managing the next batch of hires. If you start with junior people, then you're stuck as the manager. That junior person might be good at the current role, but not be able to grow into a team lead. And even if you don't have organized labor, you're violating implied seniority by hiring a manager after you already have workers. Even if you hire only one virtual assistant to do a few roles, you'll still want to have someone senior enough to manage others if you need to shift resources later.

9. Require a WSR (weekly status report):

And if they are lower wage, establish a SOD (start of day) and EOD (end of day) report to have accountability. The SOD is a live check-in like punching a time clock. EOD is 3 parts of 3 items each: what you did that day, what you're going to do tomorrow, and what you need from others (blockers)-- thus, 9 items that should take 5 minutes. In the post-COVID world, many of our staff are virtual (not the childcare workers, of course)-- but marketing, sales, and support can be. So make sure you have these expectations documented and signed as part of your employment contracts, whether freelance or in-house, in your facility or internationally.

10. Follow and encourage #LDT (Learn, Do, Teach):

Remember when we said that we can't hire someone unless there's a documented process to hire into? You'll want to encourage team members and even owners of other child care centers to be documenting repeatable processes. Ideally, have a shared pool that everyone can use. This allows us all to grow and hire together. It will help create the environment that will attract the right workers and right families, since publishing your standards builds your brand in a way that traditional marketing cannot. We've done work for Goddard corporate on their processes across all locations-- and I can tell you they put a lot of value on this component.

Dennis Yu

Dennis has been building brands and teaching marketing for over 13 years. He specializes in helping young adults grow into leaders of tomorrow by confidently developing their marketing skills through training programs and seminars with enterprise clients like The Golden State Warriors, Nike, and Rosetta Stone. None of this would be possible without the generous support of partners such as DigitalMarketer, Social Media Examiner, Fiverr, GoDaddy, Keap, OmniConvert, Onlinejobs.ph, Tom Ferry, Barry Habib and others who believe in training up millions of digital marketing professionals.

Dennis has been featured in The Wall Street Journal, New York Times, LA Times, National Public Radio, TechCrunch, Fox News, CNN, CBS Evening News and co-authored 'Facebook Nation' - a textbook taught in over 700 colleges and universities. You can contact him at dennis@blitzmetrics.com

Being a Momprenuer

Shana Issac

Do you know that moment when you just feel so overwhelmed, completely drained, and weighed down by it all? When you have a long list of to-do's for work, a family to care for at home, and your own body is screaming at you to slow down, it is exhausted. The demands never seem to stop. Is it that it really is simply all too much, to be a parent, a full-time business owner, and giving self-care to ourselves consistently? Or is there another way that you can manage your day better to be able to do it all without feeling overwhelmed?

This really hit me one weekend while I was at home working on my childcare business tasks. My middle son, 10 years old at the time , brought a game to me that I'd bought for him and his younger brother. He asked me, "Mom, will you come and play a game with us?" I said, "Okay, I'll come to play with you guys, but just let me finish up what I'm doing first. I'll be right there." So, he returned back to his room and waited patiently. After the same interaction between us a few more times.,

My son finally said, "Mom, whenever you finally come and play with us, it'll be too late."

A bit puzzled, I asked him, "So you guys aren't going to want to play the game anymore? You guys just got the game."

And he responded, "No, mom, because by the time you'll be available to play with us, we'll be too old ."

As a mom, his words crushed me! Not because they were harsh or rude, but because, unfortunately....he was right! At that moment, I decided that I had to make a change because missing out on my children's childhood moments was not an option!

As a single childcare mompreneur of 4 children, my biggest struggle was learning how to manage it all - business, home, and self. My goal of simultaneously being a great and involved mother to my children, a great CEO, and leader to my team, and a healthy and fulfilled person myself seemed so hard to achieve!

So I decided to make balancing every area of my life very intentional in order to achieve the vision of success that I wanted.

Here are 10 tips on being the CEO of each area of your life to balance it all and help drive it towards the success you desire.

1. Become the CEO of your Life

Firstly, let's clarify what a CEO actually is. A CEO is responsible for overseeing the day-to-day operations of the business or corporation. As CEO of a child-care business , most of the time, we're mompreneurs/dadpreneurs with a full plate at home that we also have to manage. In addition, on that plate, we still need to find room for ourselves. We, in essence, have three corporations: Self Corporation (YOU Inc.), Home Corporation (Home Inc.), and our Business Corporation (Dream Inc.). How does one manage them all and work well with all those responsibilities? I've personally found that having the mindset of being the CEO of each of these areas is critical as I will go into in the next 9 points.

2. Have a Vision

So first, before we can manage these corporations effectively as a CEO, we need to have a vision for each of them. What is your vision for YOU Inc.? Do you see yourself as happily married, living in your dream home? Or is your vision for yourself to be fit, healthy, and living a life of peace? What will fulfill you? What do you need to do to look after your own body? What is your vision for your Home Inc.? Is the vision of your home for it to be peaceful? Everyone getting along and the house clean? What is your vision for your Dream Inc.? Is it for you to make six figures? A million dollars? To help others? Is your vision for your childcare business to grow to 3 locations in 5 years? Having a clear vision serves as your compass and gives you a direction to move and a goal to aim for.

3. Conduct Regular Health Assessments

Now that you know the vision of where you would like to see YOU Inc., Home Inc., and Dream Inc., do an honest assessment of each and ask yourself, "How are my corporations performing? Are they performing well? Am I leading my corporations in a way that they are performing optimally?" And if not, what can I start doing today to help my three corporations achieve their best? What should you do today to get YOU Inc. to its top success? What do you need to make Home Inc. the best home possible for you and your family? What do you need to do to bring Dream Inc. to the best childcare center possible for the families, team, and children that it serves? For it to be successful and profitable? What are some things that you need to stop doing? Regular assessments of each area of your life will keep you on track on your path to true success.

4. Be the CEO of Self

The most neglected of the three corporations is usually our self-corporation or YOU, Inc. But YOU Inc. is an essential corporation because everything starts with YOU! Think of YOU Inc. as the leading overarching corporation over both of the other corporations. It assumes all of the liabilities and all of the risks. If YOU Inc. crumbles, Home Inc. and Dream, Inc. crumble. It has to be the strongest, and therefore, it is the one that needs the most time, attention, and resources. How to keep it in balance? Spend time with yourself. Pay attention to your mental and physical health. Invest in yourself. CONSISTENTLY.

Break YOU Inc. into the following departments: health, relationships, career, wealth, spirituality, and assess each area regularly. In each area of YOU Inc., ask yourself, "How am I doing?" What do I need that I'm missing? Where can I make room in my schedule to give myself what I need?

5. Home Inc.

Being a childcare mompreneur/dadpreneur is a great benefit to us in balancing work and home because most of the tasks that we have to complete at our business mimic many of the functions that we have to complete at home. That's great because we don't have to completely take off our "childcare CEO hat" to be a great CEO of Home, Inc. Home Inc. has different departments as well. We have finance, operations (cleaning, cooking, shopping, laundry, etc.), HR (managing and taking care of your family's needs, including quality time), and quality assurance, making sure everything is running efficiently. Having the mindset of looking at your home as a corporation helps you structure it so that you can run both home and business effectively and smoothly.

are high that you will get results if your whole day is set aside for related jobs or a particular project.

BONUS Tip 2 - Automate your Execution

Change only comes from taking action! It's not just about learning , but all about applying what you have learned. Therefore, as an action point for this chapter, create your own daily, weekly, and monthly action plan. Please take out a piece of paper, go back to each of these tips, and begin writing your plan to implement them into your life. Then, after completing your action plan, use it to outline your day on your Google Calendar. Use your phone alarms for reminders, and any other digital software or technology that will help you stay on point! REMEMBER: Consistency is key! For an action plan template to help you organize this all, visit www.thechildcarementher.com for an accessible template.

To achieve a great work-life balance, you have to be intentional about it. In order to fit it all in, you have to create places and boundaries in your schedule to place them in. You can do it.

Shana's Bio

From teen mom to serial entrepreneur, Shana started her first childcare business when she was 22 years old. Shana began her childcare journey in 2001 as a home childcare owner because she was a young mom who wanted to be the change that she wanted to see.

Now, as a mother of four and a multisite owner, she looks to inspire, guide, and support other mompreneurs. Shana is passionate about entrepreneurship and everything that comes with it……. the grind, the growth, the freedom, and the impact!

She loves helping ambitious female entrepreneurs and has mentored childcare owners and aspiring childcare owners on how to successfully run their childcare business to achieve the life that they desire.

MARKETING

Marketing Fundamentals

Nick Williams

In this chapter, we're going to take a look at the fundamentals of marketing that we need to have in place. Whether you're looking at generating more parent inquiries, or more potential staff, these are all essential components to have in place.

Now, I know you probably didn't go into business because you love marketing. You probably went into business because you love what you do. However, marketing is one of the five basic pillars of having a successful business, so it's really important that we at least understand the fundamentals.

I often speak to business owners that tell me they are spending money on marketing every month, but they have no idea whether it's working or not. Think about this, if you knew exactly what it costs you to acquire a new customer, wouldn't you then multiply that by the number of customers you need? So, let's take a look at all the marketing fundamentals we need to have in place.

1. Allocate the time

It's important to allocate the time to market your business each day. Now, I understand we're all stretched for time, but if you were to work an 8-hour day, that's 16 x 30 minute slots. All I'm asking you to do, is spend 1 x 30 minutes working on marketing your business. It's all about how we manage our time. Try and arrange a space where you can focus without distraction. Here's an example of how you can spend some of that time.

Follow up with inquiries.

Record a Facebook Live or pre-recorded video.

Reach out to a new contact, perhaps a local business, to build relationships.

10 minutes interacting on social media, responding to comments and interacting with local parenting groups providing value.

2. Your Ideal Customer

We need to understand exactly who is our ideal customer. I'm not just talking about knowing that they are parents or parents to be. You need to define the gender, age bracket, background, job, things they like and dislike and why they would come to you over another setting. Once you understand your ideal customer in more detail, you can then personalize your marketing accordingly. Think about it, have you ever had a customer that you just know isn't the right fit for your business. The more you can dial in your ideal customer and only attract them, the better your customer base will be and the happier you and your team will be to serve them.

Too often, businesses just use generic marketing promoting they have child care spaces available. This doesn't speak directly to their ideal customer and then end up attracting everyone and anyone. So, when you create any type of marketing from now on, think about your ideal customer and what would attract them. If you'd like more information on creating your ideal customer, be sure to get our free guide by visiting www.childcaretoptips.com/resources

3. Give staff recruitment the same focus

The same applies to staff recruitment. Too often I see basic marketing that just says, "We're Hiring Apply Now." Remember, to personalize your marketing to speak to the exact caliber of candidates you want. If you want someone with a bubbly personality and lots of experience, then say that. If you want someone that doesn't have any experience but is ambitious and determined to learn, state that in your marketing. Of course, you cannot discriminate against anyone, but you can highlight exactly what type of personality and experience you want.

4. Your elevator pitch

It's important to have an Elevator Pitch. Imagine entering a lift and your ideal customer is standing next to you on the phone trying to sort out child care. You've got 15 seconds to tell them exactly what you do and why they should use you. This is called your Elevator Pitch. Down below, you'll find a template of how to create your elevator pitch.

I help _____ by _____ to children aged __ to __.

I stand out from the competition as _____, I _____ _____ and _____ _____. Call to Action_____

Here's an example:

We help parents by providing high-quality child care to children aged 6 weeks to 4 years. We stand out from the competition as we're family run, we send you daily updates and photos of your child throughout the day, and we have the largest outdoor space in London. Would you like to arrange a tour to show you how we can help you?

Once you've created your Elevator Pitch, be sure to share it with all of your team, so you're all saying exactly the same thing to promote your business.

5. **Here are 7 Essentials to use in all your marketing materials:**

- Who it's ideal for
- Why it's beneficial for them
- What is involved
- Where it's located
- When it takes place or is available
- How they can take part
- Call to action (what do you want them to do)

6. **Google Business Profile**

This was formerly known as 'Google My Business.' It lets you manage how your child care business appears in a Google Search and on Google Maps, allowing you to add a business name, location, hours of business, photos and also reviews.

It will allow people to contact you directly, quickly and easily when you appear in a search, as well as showing all prospecting parents that you are a legitimate business.

Why it's so important for your business

- Parents who have made the certain decision they need childcare and want to use a child care center will search for terms such as "preschool in Orlando" - without having a Google Business Profile, you won't appear in that search.

- Google is the most renowned search engine used worldwide, so you need to be on it for it to work to your advantage.

- Google Business Profile is free and allows you to build a great online presence hosting: photo, video, all your important information and most importantly genuine customer reviews.

Ensuring your profile is optimized

- Upload lots of photos and videos

- Request reviews from your friends, family and clients, and always reply to them

- Ensure there is as much information as possible: Phone number, email address, location, Link to your website.

- Make sure you verify your listing.

- Add all the keywords that best describe your business to increase where you show in searches

7. Check your inquiry process

It's so important to make sure all your forms of inquiry are working correctly. Are telephone inquiries getting to you, are web forms working, are emails being responded to. Web links can break, message pads can be lost. Test them regularly to make sure the process is running smoothly.

8. Tracking your inquiries

It's important to track every inquiry and where they came from is critical if you really want to understand what marketing is working and what isn't. Of course, there are some great tools out there now that not only track all your inquiries and follow up with them automatically, they even tell you exactly where the inquiry came from, www.childcareautomation.com is a great example of this. However, if you're not ready to start using an online system yet, just get started by using a simple Excel spreadsheet and write down all your inquiries and how they heard about you. Then you can start to accurately track wherever they came from. Then you'll know exactly where to concentrate your marketing efforts.

9. How can people contact you

Be sure to offer lots of different ways people can get in contact with your business. Not everyone uses Facebook, or Whatsapp. We're now finding people prefer to text rather than pick up the phone and take a call from a number they don't recognize. Remember, someone might be working in the day, so having a text sit on their phone until they have time to respond is a great way to get more engagement from potential customers.

10. Follow up process

It's so important to always check your follow-up process. If you're using an automation service, are the tasks scheduled correctly and are you and your team completing those tasks in a timely manner. Are you continuing to follow-up weeks later if the prospect still hasn't made a decision? It's important to keep providing value and testimonials to those prospects until they either decide to buy, or tell you they're not interested anymore. Remember, people are busy, so don't give up on the inquiry too soon.

These are some of the basic marketing fundamentals that we all need to have in place. If you'd like to access more marketing tips, or you'd like to download some of our free templates, go to www.childcaretoptips.com/resources

10 Tips To Elevate Your Social Media Strategy

Nick Williams

Businesses of all shapes and sizes are using social media and of course, why wouldn't you, considering there are more than 4.5 billion users at the time of writing this chapter. That's over half of the World's population. But is being on social media enough? In this chapter, we'll take a look at 10 top tips to ensure you are following a simple strategy that allows you to be consistent regardless of how busy you are.

1. Define Your Goals

Too many people think that just being on social media, or posting the occasional post is good enough. We need to clearly define what we are looking to achieve from social media. Are you simply looking to share photos of all the great fun you have in your setting for your existing families, or are you trying to generate more inquiries. If it's just to share photos of your existing children having fun, then that's easy to do, but if it's to generate more inquiries, you need to set measurable goals around whether the content you are posting actually generates any more inquiries.

2. Who are we looking to reach and where are they

There's no point trying to post content on all platforms if all your clients are only using two major social media platforms. Just because a new social media platform comes out, doesn't mean we instantly need to abandon our existing platforms and shift all our content to the new one. Take the time to ask your existing customers what platforms do they use and why they like them.

3. What do they want to see

There's no point in creating content that no one engages with. I've seen some Facebook pages with 118,000 followers, but an average post they put out on social media only gets between 8 - 10 likes per post. If you want to create content that resonate with your audience, you need to know what they care about the most. Take the time to ask your audience what type of content they'd like to see.

4. Plan out your content

Let's face it, you already have enough on your plate to not want to worry about finding time to post on social media every day. By preparing your content in advance, you'll not only save time, but you'll be sure never to miss anything.

Make a list of upcoming festivals and special days you celebrate

Create a content theme to provide your audience with a unified experience

Prepare a list of hashtags for different social media platforms

Look at using a content calendar, so you can schedule all your content in advance

5. Optimize Your Bios

Adding keywords to your bio will help you show up more often in search results. Include phrases that your audience will be searching for – Childcare in 'your area,' Childcare options, Best Childcare in 'your area.' Encourage Check-ins. You could design a simple backdrop that encourages people to take selfies or share photos on Instagram and Facebook. You could run competitions rewarding parents for the most shares, or the best selfie pic using your custom backdrop.

6. Run Competitions

There are plenty of people you could ask for freebies from - suppliers or local businesses, particularly those looking to promote their services to your audience. Plan out a competition at least once a month and relate it to a theme going on at that time. You could encourage your parents to create something with their child at home and share it with your group. Then you can respond and tag them in so all their friends and family can see.

7. Promote Your Audience Not You

We all love a bit of praise from others, particularly when our friends and family get to see it. So help them out! Congratulate parents and carers for taking part

Dollar a Day: The Ultimate Digital Hack

Dennis Yu

Even with great reviews, awesome staff that really care for the children, the most modern facilities, and the best location-- you probably still have marketing as the greatest pain point. That's because the referral channels are moving to digital, which includes social channels like TikTok. Did you know that TikTok went from the 7th most popular website in 2021 to #1 in 2022, ahead of Google? And that 40% of users are over 30 years old and growing?

Even if the waiting list to get into your daycare is 3 months long, you'll still want to be visible, sharing helpful tips, and doing things other than just lead generation. The "Dollar A Day" strategy is how you ensure that all parents in your city, no matter if they are on Google, TikTok, YouTube, or any other channel, know about you and your brand.

Let's go through 10 points on how to implement Dollar a Day for your childcare center:

1. First, collect your positive mentions:

If you have a virtual assistant or agency that is already doing this, great. You can budget 4-5 hours of effort if you're an established business to organize and collect these items across Facebook, Google Business Profile, Yelp, YouTube, the general web, your website, and elsewhere. Assume $50 to get this into a Google sheet, one row per mention, showing date, link, authority level, type of content, who is being featured, and your notes.

2. Pull out the video mentions

If you've been interviewed on podcasts, have your own podcast, spoken on stage, been on TV, or done webinars, then you can yank out these snippets in a new tab within your sheet called "video mentions". I like Descript for editing, since it has built in transcription, editing, and other bits- so you can edit the videos ad simply as editing the words. Apple Clips and even the native TikTok video editor are great, but don't do a good job resizing to vertical video (9x16), which is what we need on Facebook. If you have your own video editor or hire them on Fiverr or Upwork, then they are probably using Premiere Pro, which could potentially cost you money unnecessarily and also create stuff that blatantly looks like an ad. Put a closing bumper with your center's name and map location. Have your opening bumper play AFTER the initial 3-second hook (attention getter), since opening with your bumper (even if your designer thinks the logo and words flying across the screen is nice) kills the video.

3. Post the top mentions to your Facebook page.

This means your company page and a public figure page if you have it. And we recommend you do create one if you don't. See mine at fb.com/getfound for a decent example. Don't worry about "spreading out" the posts. Facebook shows your posts to only 2% of your fans anyway, so just make a bunch of posts. If you're a major brand, then perhaps schedule it. Make your posts honoring the parent, community member, podcast host, local organization, or whoever is talking about you. Upload the video directly, not as a YouTube link or whatever, since Facebook will kill your reach if you do, it's like driving a Honda to the Toyota dealership. Ideally, you have 10-20 posts to start, which have a different mix of scenes and topics, as opposed to 20 clips from the same video.

4. Boost the Facebook post

You can do it right from the timeline using the big blue "boost post" button. Put a dollar a day against each post for 7 days. So if you have 20 posts, you're spending $140 to test this initial batch. Target a 5-mile radius of your childcare center. Don't target by demographics, though tempting to try to target parents with children of certain ages. The big algo shift is that targeting is going away, since Facebook is doing the targeting for you. In other words, Facebook looks at who is engaging to find similar people. And when you run conversion objective campaigns, they automatically optimize to the lowest cost per conversion-without you needing to include custom audiences or lookalikes.

5. Post and boost on Twitter

Doing the same as on Facebook, upload the videos natively with a short caption, targeting only the geo. Twitter's boosting also drives engagement, where you select the organic tweet at the last step. Run at $1 a day if you've got just one tweet. Or you can bucket 10 of them into a single ad set (simply checking more tweets from the list) at perhaps $5 a day. Your cost per engagement will be much lower than Facebook, but you'll get fewer clicks. You could choose clicks as the objective, which will give you cheaper clicks, but then your reach and pass-along engagement go down. In other words, boosting for engagement gives you a nice multiplier if your video is interesting. The 1,000 people you pay to reach for perhaps $7 could give you an additional 2,000 reach for free because of the "discount factor" or reward you get for behaving nicely. Likewise, if your engagement is low or if people mark your ad as spam, Twitter will raise your prices and potentially disable your account,

6. Repeat on other channels

You can apply the same techniques on Snapchat, LinkedIn, TikTok, YouTube, and other networks. Except instead of a dollar a day, you must spend $5 a day to test on Snapchat, $10 a day on LinkedIn, and $20 a day on TikTok. YouTube will work at $1 a day, but you need to be more sophisticated about the videos that you run, since viewers on YouTube expect more depth, longer form content, and higher production value. You could run 6 second bumper ads on YouTube and even lead ads on LinkedIn. But I recommend you get solid campaigns going on Facebook and Twitter before going to other networks.

7. Analyze the results.

Don't make the fatal mistake of not going back to analyze results, which is what most people do. Out of every 10 posts, generally you'll find one "winner" that outperforms all the others by a lot. Usually that post has more than a 10% engagement rate, which corresponds to a lower CPM (cost per thousand impressions) and lower cost of everything else. Now put $2 a day against that winner for 14 more days. And then extend for $3 a day for a month, and so forth, until your ad frequency gets above 2 per month, your performance begins to decline, or you have more leads than you can handle. We've seen local businesses with boosted posts that have been running for 6 years. These posts are what we call our "Greatest Hits", which will continue to record forever. But be sure that you don't burn them out by having a budget too high to allow them to run forever. Customer success stories, your knowledge, and anything else you share on social as a story are "evergreen" content by design. So that you can be driving steady leads (even with seasonality) even if you don't make any new campaigns or don't have fresh content.

8. Harvest your content

Don't just stop with the initial inventory to collect mentions. When you've boosted posts on multiple networks, you will see parents will comment. These are leads you must monitor and respond to— often in the form of simple questions that lead to a call and in-person visit. You will get more positive mentions, too, which you can cycle back into your ad campaigns. Most businesses don't bother to look at ad comments, which means missing out on gold and sometimes allowing a negative comment to sit unaddressed for quite some time.

9. Give birth to "unicorn children"

Larry Kim, founder of WordStream, which was the highest spending agency on the planet with 2% of Google's total spend and 2% of Facebook's total spend said that when you find a winner (unicorn), you should then give birth to unicorn children. What he means by that is to examine what made a post take off or convert well, then doing something similar. Maybe you have a shot of children on the playground outside that was a winner. Try it with different children. Create other shots on the equipment. Re film it on the latest iPhone. Try different background music. Adjust the color of the buttons. Change the call to action. Of course, don't have the next video with 10 differences at once, since then you can't isolate which factor made the difference. This is where you need a strong sense of strategy to be able to test one or two things at a time, playing the "winner stay on" strategy.

10. Steal (I mean, copy) from your competitors

Facebook, Google, and TikTok let us see what ads competitors are running - sometimes even how much they're spending and who they are targeting. The longer the ad had been running and the more money being spent, the more likely it's a winner for them. I like to get inspiration by seeing the general theme they're using, then film our version of it. If you find that your remake isn't performing as well as you'd like, check out your landing page (native lead ads or web page), see if your team is responding to leads within 5 minutes, listen to call disposition to see if they're not handling leads properly, and check the digital plumbing (tracking) to see if it's a data/code issue.

That's the 10-step process to run the Dollar a Day Strategy for childcare centers.

I hope you found this not only interesting, but also highly profitable for you on an on-going basis. Thank you to Nick for inviting me to write this chapter.

The Importance of Brand Development

Kimberley Taylor

Not sure about the meaning of "branding"? Don't worry! The phrase "on brand/branding" is very vague and is often misunderstood and misused, this is because it is reduced to the atheistic components, e.g. your logo. Whilst many people concentrate on the visual identity of a company (name, logo, packaging) there are several other essential components that make up a successful brand.

Branding is essentially a pattern of familiarity that exists in people's minds, often connected to an emotional response. Everything we know about the services or products we use is because of branding. It is the link that connects the company to the customer.

By having a branding strategy, you have a long-term plan to achieve a series of goals that ultimately allow you to distinguish yourself from your competitors and clarify what it is you offer that makes you the better choice. A successful branding strategy encompasses the brand's mission, its promises to its customers and therefore sets the parameters for expectations, and how these are communicated. Your brand is built to be a true representation of who you are as a business, and how you wish to be perceived.

Your Brand Strategy sums up why your business exists beyond making sales.

Here are my top 10 tips for creating a brand strategy: -

1. Audience personas (Customer avatar)

Your Audience Personas (customer avatar) should be an example of your customer base. These fictional profiles will help to ensure your brand and marketing will appeal to your audience. By documenting your customer personas, you are showing people the type of customers you want to attract. Typically, you will include elements such as age, gender, location, spending habits, pain points, factors in purchasing decisions, reading and social media habits.

2. Competitor research

It is always important to carry out competitor research. By taking an in-depth look into the competitive landscape, you begin to understand where you sit and how you can grow to exceed customer expectations. Always look at a mix of local, national, and international competitors, see what they offer, and profile any key insights that help your brand (especially things they are not doing well). This will allow you to identify how you can do them better, hence making you stand out.

3. Brand positioning

Brand positioning is the process of placing your brand in the mind of your customers, it creates clarity around who you serve, it helps to differentiate your brand amongst its competitors, reflecting your core brand values through your communication channels. Within your brand guidelines, you should outline how you are doing that. To create your brand positioning statement, use the following formula:

[Brand Name]'s [offering] is the only [category/service/product] that [benefit you bring to your customers].

4. Brand story

Your brand story is unique to you – it can be funny, unexpected, serious, ambitious… but one thing is for sure, it must spark an emotional reaction. It wants to focus on how you help your customers. By including your brand story, it can help you connect with your audience - whether they have been in the same situation, can empathize with it or it may be an inspiration to them. The brand story will not only help with the connection, but also gives you a stronger foundation in your positioning.

5. Brand values

At the core of your brand strategy, you will find your brand values. This collection of words should have an impact. They are imperative to every aspect of your business, not just your marketing materials. They help set the tone of your company and can help give customers an insight to who you are. Remember words like honest and reliable, can sometimes have a negative impact, your audience expects these things as standard, if you have to point them out, these things could be questioned. Instead, think about your unique values, try writing down 20 words that define your company values, get others involved, then reduce the list to the top 5.

6. Brand mission

Some people call it a brand mission, others a vision or a purpose. Mission is apt, because just like sending a man to the moon, you're answering the question, "Where are we aiming to be?" By having a brand mission even if it changes over time, you have a clear direction of where you are aiming to go and what you are looking to achieve, this will help identify the steps you need to take to achieve your mission.

7. A brand touchpoint

A brand touchpoint is the place and time where a customer comes in contact with your brand. Touchpoints can be tricky to document in your brand guidelines. Think about your brand from an in-person point of view and a digital perspective. Make a list of the user experience touchpoints from the first time they see your brand, to meeting you and then follow up. Making a list that documents how and when customers will come into contact with your brand can be useful. Once you have the list you can then look at these touchpoints in more depth, to ensure they meet the standards of your brand guides and allow your brand to be seen and experienced in the best possible way.

8. Brand messaging

Your brand messaging is "what" you're trying to communicate, and how you communicate it. It is a framework on which you can base all your external communications. This helps ensure there is continuity in the things that you are saying as a brand. Having continuity will not only help with brand recognition, but also how you are positioned in the minds of your customers. Having consistent messaging gives a brand a stable and trustworthy presence.

9. Your tone of voice

Brand voice is not only *what* you say to your audience, but also *how* you say it. Brand tone is the mood or emotion you articulate in messaging, through specific word choices and writing styles. Essentially, it's how you express your brand, it's your brands personality. Examples of this are the way you greet people or sign off on messages e.g. Do you greet people with; Hi, hey, hello or howdy...? In a crowded market visual components help you stand out, but your written content needs the same attention and consistency you give to other elements. Brand voice plays a significant role in storytelling, personality and memorable content, these all play a massive role in helping you stand out from the competition and having an impact on your customers.

10. Brand Visual Identity

Brand identity is the visual elements of a brand including, logos, typography, colors, packaging, and messaging, that distinguish and identify a brand, essentially it's the way your communication looks to your audience. It can complement and reinforce the reputation of your brand. Think about if you want your brand to look fun, serious, strong. All of these words would have a difference in brand aesthetics. Think about typography, ensure the style of letter format represents your brand well and is functional (is it easy to ready on lots of platforms by lots of people). When choosing a color palette, look at simple color theory (see table below). Research shows that people decide if they like a product within 90 seconds, 90% of that is based on color. The most important thing to remember is that your visuals represent you, and they have a massive impact on customers, keeping continuity in style and look will help with recognition and trust. If in doubt - keep it simple! One of the most recognizable and most trusted brands is Ford motor company, their first logo was created in 1909 featuring only the word "ford" as an imitation of Henry Ford's handwriting, whilst it has changed several times over the years, the basis of the simple handwritten word is still part of the brand today.

Red	Passion, Love, Anger, hunger, immediacy, sale
Blue	Trust, smart, calm,faith, natural, stable, power
Black	Bold, rich, mystery, elegance, strength, evil
Green	Soothing, eco-friendly, natural, envy, jealousy, balance, restful
Yellow	Cheer, attention, childish, warmth, energy, optimism
Orange	Health, attraction, standout, thirst, wealth, youthful, happiness
pink	Tenderness, sensitive, caring, emotional, sympathetic, love
purple	Royal, mysterious, arrogant, luxury, childish, creative, sadness
white	Purity, cleanliness
brown	Nature, wholesomeness, dependability

Good design can make or break your first impression with website visitors. So, take the time to really work on your brand, as it's a representation of you and your business and what you stand for.

Kimberley is Head of Design and brand at Childcare Business Growth. Be sure to check out some of Kim's other articles and videos by visiting www.childcare-businessgrowth.com

SALES

How to Build a Profitable Childcare Business, Using Disney Style Marketing

Andrew Lock

You obviously know Disney. Everyone does. But why should your childcare business model Disney? Two simple and important reasons. First, they are one of the most *profitable* companies in the world. They're obviously doing a lot of things right. Secondly, they're one of the most *respected* companies in the world. It's extremely rare to be both profitable and deeply admired, it's something of a magical combination. With that, let's dive into the 10 marketing lessons...

1: Everything is Marketing, and Marketing is Everything

Walt Disney said *"Do what you do so well that they (your customers) will want to come back again and bring their friends!"*

That simple quote shows that Walt understood marketing on a deep level.

Here's how I describe marketing:

"Marketing is <u>anything</u> you or your employees do

that affects other people's view of your business."

In other words it's *everything* you do in your childcare business that affects how people view you. Marketing is an incredibly powerful force.

At Disney, a cast member (employee) may be assigned to clean the bathrooms, be a security guard, or a ride operator, but their **primary** role is to help guests (which is marketing, because marketing is anything that affects people's view of the business).

So the first lesson is to recognize that in order to be successful, you have to change your own view of your business. *First and foremost,* if you want to have a successful business over the long-term, you must *view yourself as a marketer. You are a marketer.*

2: Offer Unique Products

In Disney theme parks, they try not to sell anything that you can buy outside the parks. This is strategic, and by design.

Why?

There's a marketing principle called the 'apples to apples' comparison. This is a psychological principle where a customer *already* knows the approximate cost of an item because its readily available everywhere. They make an immediate comparison to other times they've purchased the same item.

For example, everyone knows the price of a can of Coke. When offered a Coke, your brain can't help but make the immediate 'apples to apples' comparison to other times you've bought a coke, such as at a supermarket, restaurant, bar, or vending machine.

The reason this is a problem in business is that there's an inherent price barrier, based on assumption.

Although Disney still sells Coke products, they're steering the business away from doing that, because there's far more profit to be had in selling *unique* products.

For example, at Gaston's Tavern in the *Magic Kingdom* park, the only drink available is called *Le Fou's Brew*. It's a non-alcoholic concoction of frozen apple juice, with a hint of toasted marshmallow, topped with a passion-fruit and mango flavored foam. It's delicious!

For guests it's a fun experience to try unique drinks, and for Disney they make far more money because the drinks are sold at premium prices (3-4x the cost of a Coke).

What can you offer your customers that makes you unique, so that they can't do an apples to apples comparison?

3: Make It *Easy* to Buy!

At the Disney theme parks, they've implemented a number of things to make it easy for guests to spend money in the stores. An example is how they've taken the walls down between adjacent stores, allowing guests to roam freely between them. This is genius.

What's the underlying marketing *principle* here?

Simply, *make it easy for customers to buy!*

Far too often, companies unwittingly sabotage their own business by placing barriers in the way of a sale. An example is how the checkout process of many websites force customers to create an account before they can do anything else. That's a barrier to the sale, because a big long form asking for lots of personal details is intimidating and frustrating, causing many prospects to click away because they don't want the hassle.

Look at your child care business closely and see if you can identify any barriers that you're currently placing in the way of making the sale. For example, do you ask parents to fill in paperwork that asks for repeated information like name / address on multiple pages? Could the forms be simplified or pre-filled with known information? Would it be easier to have them filled out on a tablet? Again, try to minimize or eliminate any frustrating barriers to the sale.

4: Use Upsells

Do you know the number one time to persuade a customer to spend more money? It's immediately after the sale! It takes a lot for someone to commit to a purchase, but once they've reached that point it's far easier for them to add other items to the transaction.

An upsell is the process of offering a customer *a larger quantity of an item, an upgraded or premium version of the item, or a relevant related item.*

Perhaps the most famous example of an upsell is how McDonalds staff ask, *"Would you like fries with that?"*

When a guest approaches the ticket window at a Disney theme park, the signage indicates a variety of upsells: a higher number of days at the parks, a 'park-hopper' option, or the addition of a water-park. These upsells dramatically increase the profitability of the business.

Within the parks, a common upsell option is a souvenir mug. You can opt for a regular drink, or elect to have it in a commemorative collectible souvenir mug. Obviously these mugs are visually appealing and as a result many guests choose to upgrade their order.

The key to success with upsells in your childcare business is to strategize what can be offered, and then implement a system so that every customer is consistently offered the upsell(s).

5: Use Scarcity

The marketing principle of 'scarcity' is all about limiting the availability of an item. That can be done by limiting the number of units available, or the time that it's available.

When Disney were focusing on selling DVD's, they used scarcity effectively by telling customers, *"Pickup this timeless classic movie before it goes back into the Vault."* Of course, there was no actual vault, but limiting the time the movie was available forced people to make a decision about buying it.

And that's the point. Scarcity forces customers to avoid procrastinating or thinking, "I can get this later." You need to give them a compelling reason to buy *now*, rather than later.

Note that scarcity should be positioned as a *positive benefit of acting fast*; it shouldn't involve intimidation or high pressure selling. Also, always give a *valid* & legitimate *reason* for the scarcity, or you will lose credibility.

A natural scarcity in your childcare business is most likely a limit on the number of children you can accept. That's a good one to leverage. In your marketing you can say you only have x spots available, and once they're gone, they're gone.

6: Maximizing Profits Through Special Events

Within the first few years of *Disneyland's* opening, Walt quickly realized that the local population in Southern California made up the vast majority of visitors. So, he regularly met with his management team to discuss creative ways to *keep the locals coming back*.

The key turned out to be special events.

First, they implemented 'Date Night' on Friday and Saturday nights, where the park would stay open much later, until midnight. They brought in a big band orchestra, and a special ticket included admission for 2 people.

Later, Disney arranged special concerts inside Disneyland featuring big name artists at the time, including The Osmonds, The Carpenters, and Glen Campbell.

These days, special events are a central strategy at all parks, such as the hugely popular graduation events at Disneyland, the food and wine festival at Epcot, and the Star Wars weekends at Disney's Hollywood Studios. Throughout the year, special events are regularly scheduled.

Throughout the year there are numerous holidays you can tie-into, like St Patrick's Day, Mardi Gras, and New Year's Eve. Create a marketing calendar and think about creative ways to tie-in to the chosen theme.

7: Creating Loyalty

Every human wants to feel and be treated as someone special. In your business, *regular* customers particularly deserve to be recognized and treated as special. Sadly, in most businesses they're not.

Disney offers their most frequent customers the 'annual pass' option which provides a substantial discount, along with many other perks and benefits such as free parking.

I enjoy using Hotels.com specifically because of their loyalty program. For every ten nights cumulatively booked at any hotels, Hotels.com rewards me with a free night. It's great, because I don't need to be loyal to one specific hotel brand. I can pick any hotel brand for each booking, and still be rewarded for making the bookings via Hotels.com.

Whatever you decide, keep your loyalty program simple, and try to avoid complex legal jargon or small print. A loyalty program should be easily understood, and it should *genuinely* reward customers, rather than making them jump through hoops to claim the benefits!

8: Language Matters!

Walt placed high importance on the choice of words used within the business, and he tried to educate employees about that at every opportunity.

For example, he referred to customers as *'guests'*, because he knew that guests are treated much better than customers. You have *transactions* with *customers*, whereas you welcome and personally look after *guests*. Likewise, *'customer'* is a fairly generic word, and it tends to conjure up an image of a faceless, random person, who is just one of many, whereas *'guest'* conveys more of a valued and personal relationship.

I often hear workers refer to the 'price' or 'cost' of something. However, a much better word to use is *'investment,'* because it changes the buyers thought process, from *cost* to *benefit*.

Another word I'd like to see eliminated from employees vocabulary, is *'problem.'* It's a negative word that triggers a negative mindset. Why not replace it with the word *'challenge'* instead? A 'challenge' is something that has a more positive connotation, because it reminds us that we can do something about it. We have a choice. By contrast, 'problem' sounds much more pessimistic.

If you work in a customer service role, how much better to respond to customers with *"You're welcome"* or *"My pleasure!"* Can you see how much better those expressions are?

If your childcare business involves a contract or agreement, it's best to refer to it as *'paperwork'*, as in "lets fill in the paperwork" rather than saying, *"let's get you to sign the contract"*. See the difference? These details relate back to marketing, and they matter!

9: Create a Memorable Experience

Most businesses focus on transactions: a simple exchange of a product or service, for money.

There's two big problems with that. First, your business is instantly forgettable, and second, you open yourself up to competition as soon as someone comes along offering a cheaper price.

So, your goal should always be to create a positive, memorable experience. Aim to surprise and delight customers so that they think to themselves (or even better tell others), *"Wow! That was amazing!"*

On one occasion a few weeks after the opening of Disneyland, a gardener approached Walt in a panic, and said, *"Walt, look at this! We need to install a fence, because people are walking on the grass to take pictures of the Sleeping Beauty castle!"*

Without hesitation, Walt said, *"The guests are absolutely right, that's a great place to take photos. What we need is a path to make it easier for them!"*

Can you see the difference in attitude? Walt genuinely cared about his guests, and always gave them the highest priority, rather than focusing on what would be best for himself or the company. It wasn't that the gardener was wrong to care about the grass and flowers, but he had missed the *bigger* picture of *why* he was doing those things – for the guest experience.

Sometimes we can get so close to our own business that we start to see customers as an annoyance, or something to be tolerated, rather than valued. By contrast, our goal should be to design an experience so that customers are so impressed they tell their friends and come back over and over again.

10: Attention to Details

Walt famously said, *"When we consider a new project, we really study it; not just the surface idea, but everything about it."*

One of the key ways Walt achieved this was by having incredible attention to the details. It's no exaggeration to say that he knew every corner of Disneyland, and he was obsessed about the details.

As an example, Walt would sometimes buy a hotdog from a cart in a random spot of the park, casually walk and eat the hotdog, and note the exact spot where he finished eating. If there was no trash can within easy reach, he would immediately arrange for one to be installed in that area. Later, trash cans were installed throughout the parks, within about twenty-five steps of each other.

If a guest approaches a cast member to ask for directions, the cast member will always point with two fingers and an open palm. Try it and see for yourself. Why do they do this? First, they realized that it tends to make your arm straighter for clearer directions, and second, in some countries it's considered rude to point with one finger. Again, *every* little detail is thought out.

As guests walk around the parks, they may detect various subtle scents in the air. For example, outside the bakery and ice-cream stores on Main Street there's the sweet smell of fresh-baked cookies. As you stroll through *Frontierland* it smells old and musty. This is no accident. To distribute scents around the park Disney uses a device that imagineers invented and patented, called a *Smellitzer*. Yes, every little detail is thought out.

Do you give this level of attention to detail in your business? Or are most things left to chance? For example, customers should never see stacks of boxes, trash, employees smoking, eating, or arguing.   Those things *should* be obvious, because they negatively impact the guest experience, but you'd be amazed how few businesses get even these fundamentals right. Again, because these things directly affect the customer's view of your business, they come under the category of marketing.

If you've enjoyed this snapshot into the many lessons to be learned from Disney, I encourage you to read the book "Walt Disney's Way," which goes into much more depth about how business owners can 'Disnify' their business to stand out from the crowd, and ultimately make more money. You can find the book on Amazon, or visit: www.TheWaltDisneyBook.com

Building A Dream 100 & Community Marketing

Nick Williams

In this chapter, we're going to take a look at the ways to market our business by leveraging our relationships with local businesses and the wider community.

1. Dream 100

Your ideal customer is already someone else's customer. So, they're already buying products or services from someone else. They could be a mother to be going to prenatal classes with a personal trainer, or they could be buying baby clothes from your local clothes store. They could be an existing parent taking their child to an indoor play center. These businesses become part of my Dream 100 List.

They are all businesses that already have my ideal customer and I want to create a relationship with that business, so if their customer is ever looking for childcare, they'll recommend me.

Here are some examples of who might be on your dream 100 list - gyms, salons, toy stores, blog writers, doctors, play centers, dentists, mother and toddler groups, children's hair salons, estate agents. Basically, any business that already has your ideal customer and doesn't offer the same product or service as you. Building a relationship with these dream 100 list is key to getting them referring to your business.

2. Contact Large Local Businesses

Getting your services listed on the employee benefits program is a great way of potentially accessing a lot of parents. They may already have a solution in place, but acting as their overflow is still a great opportunity. The employer will be looking at why they should partner with you, so having an exclusive offer is going to be key to selling the program to the decision makers. Another important factor is making sure that your package is right for them. Think about hospitals for example, or factory workers. They have lots of parents working unsociable hours, so can you offer a flexible package for them. Schools are another scenario, because they may only want childcare during the school term. Once you've got a partnership in place, you really want to try to arrange a presentation to anyone interested perhaps during their lunch hour, or they may invite you along to employer fairs. Make sure you take plenty of professional marketing and have your offer ready to present. This probably isn't going to be something that happens overnight, but you never know, you may call an employer at the right time when they're looking for a solution.

3. Medical Professionals

Do you ask on your enrollment forms for medical information, including doctors and dentists names and locations? You can tell parents that you need the information in case of an emergency. You may find that a lot of your families use the same dentist, so it would be great to form a partnership with them. Approach the dentist and let them know that a number of children from their practice come to your setting, and you'd like to work with them to ensure you're doing everything possible to promote healthy teeth. This way it shows the dentist that you're setting is very popular with their patients and that you care about the health of the children's teeth. Why not invite them or one of their colleagues in to deliver a talk to all your parents and children. That way, they also get to meet other potential parents at your setting. You could start this relationship by delivering a parcel of fresh fruit and a note explaining the message above. Make sure you follow this up if you haven't heard from them.

4. Partner with Local Estate Agents

If people are moving to the area, they may not yet be aware of the childcare options around them. So partnering with local estate agents gives you the opportunity to impress them even before they've moved in. You could offer a special rate exclusively for moving day. It helps make the estate agent look great for arranging it for them, and it gives you an opportunity to impress the parents right from the start. You could also offer an exclusive package for the first month. Approach the estate agents by taking in a nice gift, it could be some freshly baked cookies from you to sweeten them up, and make sure you approach them in person and not just via a phone call.

5. Photographers & Wedding Venues

You may already be bringing in a photographer to take pictures of your children, but what about them promoting you in return. You could offer them a cash incentive for each referral, or the opportunity to be on your membership card to encourage parents to use them. Whatever you do, make sure it's trackable so you can thank the right person.

If there are any wedding venues nearby, you can approach them and offer your services as a wedding crèche. This is not only a great opportunity for you to promote your business to parents attending the event, but it can provide a great additional revenue stream for you. We got started by offering our services for free for one wedding to a local wedding venue. They were so pleased with the results that they now recommend us to all the weddings held at the venue.

Community Marketing

There are so many opportunities to develop relationships with your local community, and the great thing is, it's going to cost you hardly anything except time, but will bring you a great return on your investment. How great would it feel if someone new to your community asked about where to find the best childcare and everyone highly recommended you? That's the benefit of community marketing, so let's take a look at how you can develop these relationships.

6. Free Friends Day or Free Training Days

Invite your customers to bring a friend on a traditionally quieter day of the week where you can host a stay and play session. Make sure you collect their contact information to follow up and present them with an offer. The same can apply to free training days. If you're putting on a first aid course for your team, why not invite some local parents to join the first aid course for free. It's a great way to build relationships and get people talking about you.

7. Contact Local Groups

There are usually lots of groups that already have your ideal customers attending them, stay and play groups and parent clubs. You could contact them and ask to pop along to introduce your setting. If you're more confident, you could offer to do a talk on a particular topic that's relevant to them. Sourcing these groups is one job that could be passed on to a virtual assistant. If you'd like to get our guide on hiring a virtual assistant, visit www.childcaretoptips.com/resources

8. Partnering with your local library

Ok libraries aren't as popular as they used to be, but a large number of parents and children still use them, and they often tend to invite schools and childcare settings in for activities. So let the library know how much you appreciate them by regularly taking them some tasty treats and giving them some flowers. If other childcare practitioners are using them, then you need to stand out from the crowd and go those ten steps further to make them feel that extra bit special. So, the next time anyone asks them which childcare setting they'd recommend, it will be you coming to the front of mind. Don't forget to include lots of promotional materials to leave them on the counter.

9. Partner with local schools

If parents have children attending school, then there's a good chance they may also have a younger child. Putting on talks or workshops for parents at the school is a great way to reach a large number of people that may need your services, or know several other people looking for childcare. Teachers are another great example. Why not create a term time offer exclusively for teachers. We do this every year with our local schools, and the Principals always support us by putting up flyers and posters and personally handing out letters to teachers who may be looking to return to work following the birth of their child. Another way to further show your support for the local schools is to help out at local gatherings. Again, make the most of the opportunity with your own brand of clothing, lots of promotional material and a competition to gather everyone's details.

10. Partner with local Colleges and Universities.

There are some great ways to build relationships with them. First of all, their staff may need childcare, so put in place an exclusive discount purely for that College or University. Try and get a slot where you can get to stand in front of them and tell them about your amazing setting. You may find students are looking for childcare. The ideal opportunity would be to sit down with the Principal or Dean to arrange an exclusive discount and the student funding support. It's far better to do this face to face with the decision makers and then arrange to present your setting, either via a live face to face presentation, or a pre-recorded webinar that they can watch at their convenience. You may struggle to get the College or University to exclusively work with you promoting your programs, but you could offer the Principal / or Dean a partnership; for every student that brings their child to your setting, you offer one of their students a work placement in exchange. The leadership board will be happy with this if they see that their learners are securing a work placement opportunity with each referred enrollment.

These ideas are just a small sample taken from our book 207 Ways To Market Your Childcare Business, so if you'd like more ideas, be sure to get your free copy of the book.

10 Tips To The Perfect Tour

Nick Williams

In this chapter, we're going to take a look at how to conduct the perfect tour and how you can stand out from your competition.

I know it may sound obvious, but let's take a look at why the tour is so important.

- The parent has liked you online or over the phone, and taken the time to reach out to you, and now they want to spend the time to get you know you more. Remember, they probably have lots of choice, and you're one setting that they've chosen to take the time to visit.

- It's the key moment for the parent to check if your values, approach, set-up and personality match what they had in mind for their child.

- It's your time to give a magical experience - they will tell other parents about how it went and how you made them feel.

We're going to look at everything from conducting the tour, to how you should ask for the enrollment and then the follow-up. You may have seen some of these points from our book, *207 Ways To Market Your Child Care Business*, but it's worthwhile going back over them.

I'd encourage you to check yourself off against each one of these and give yourself a rating of 0 - 5. 0 = Not doing at all, right the way up to 5 = fully in place and happy. That way you can always come back and check your progress against each point.

1. Pre tour call

It's really important to conduct a pre tour call. Parents forget things, and I'm sure you've had a few occasions where someone has forgotten to turn up.

- Use the call to remind them and check they're coming.
- Show lots of enthusiasm (and avoid sounding desperate).

- Tell them you're looking forward to meeting them.
- Give them an idea about what they might expect.

Remember, some parents won't answer the call, so be sure to use their preferred communication method, such as text messages.

2. Make it a sensory experience

Think about the last time you walked into a new restaurant and how you created your first impressions of that business. First, you may have judged them on how it looked from the outside. Did it look clean and welcoming? Then, as you walked in, you would have been hit by the smell. Did the smell of delicious food excite you, or was there a smell of burnt food in the air. What did it sound like? Was it loud with great music, or was it so quiet you could hear a pin drop. Did you have to stand up to wait for a table, or did you have a comfy sofa to enjoy some pre-dinner drinks? Finally, the food, how did it taste, was it warm, did it fill you up. I'm sure you can relate to those sensations. Guess what, the same applies to when someone is viewing your setting. They are judging you on all of these senses, but it's even more important because it's for their child.

So use the following to see how you do against the five senses:

SIGHT - What do people see as they approach your setting and when they enter the building. Is it bright and colorful, clean and tidy, and somewhere you'd like to send your child.

SMELL - As you open the door, what does it smell like? Is it fresh, musky, or is there a hint of dirty nappy in the air.

SOUND - Have you got calming or happy music playing, or are you drowned out by the sound of babies crying.

TASTE - Do you provide your prospects with a drink and perhaps some freshly cooked biscuits from the kitchen before the tour.

TOUCH - Have you got somewhere comfortable for the prospect to sit when they come in, or are they stuck standing in the hall.

All these senses have a considerable impact on your prospect's first impressions of you and your business, so it's important to regularly assess yourself against these and always be looking for ways you can improve on them.

3. First Impressions Count

So, we've covered off the five senses on the initial first impressions, but it doesn't stop there. Now it's time for the tour to begin, so here are some suggestions to assess yourself against -

1. Are the children happy ?

2. Are your team members happy and interacting with the children?

3. Are they presentable and welcoming when you introduce them to the prospect ?

4. Are your display boards up-to-date and representing what you're currently doing in the setting?

5. Have you got a display board purely for parent updates ?

6. Are you readdressing their concerns or questions that they raised in the initial assessment?

7. Is the outdoor space well maintained and all the equipment in a good condition?

8. Do you have all your certificates on show ?

9. Have you pointed out the things that make your setting unique (and the benefits to the customer)?

10. Is there lots of evidence that your setting is a fun, family-friendly place?

4. Make them feel special

I like the saying, "Raise your hand as high as you can, and stretch that bit further." Think about all the ways you can make the tour that little more special and personal. One way to do this is to have a personalized welcome greeting in your reception area.

5. Use their name

It's important to use their name throughout the tour, as it helps build a stronger relationship with the parent and child. Make sure all your team know the name of the parent and child, as it will help portray a lot more confidence to the parent. According to research, hearing our name lights up different parts of our brain that no other words do.

6. Have your questions and answers ready.

Have you ever been asked a question, but you don't know the answer? It can be a little embarrassing, so it's important to prepare ahead of time.

Prepare which questions you'll ask the parent to get the information you need.

Ensure you are confident with the questions they might ask - keep rehearsing them.

It's also important to ensure your team know the answers too. Take the time to ask your team for questions they get asked and ensure they are all answering them the same.

7. Find out exactly what they are looking for in a setting.

Think about it, when you go to buy a car, they don't show you every car in the showroom. They sit you down and find out exactly what you're looking for first. Of course, finding childcare is nothing like buying a car, but everyone is potentially looking for something different. Some parents may focus on the curriculum, or the quality of care, whereas others may just want their child to have fun and get as much fresh air as possible. Take the time to listen to the parent. Some parents will tell you that they've never been asked that question before on other tours, so you're already ahead of the competition by taking the time to ask. Once you know what they're looking for, you can personalize the tour to address the points they've raised.

8. Nurture relationships.

While you are giving a parent a tour of your setting, it's important to give them time to talk with the key members of staff that will be responsible for their child, so they get the time to start to develop a relationship with them. Remember, this is a huge trust based decision, so allowing extra time during the tour to spend with these key people is going to help build that trust.

Allow them to trial the food and meet the cook and introduce them to other key members of your team like your parent partnership coordinator. Yes, your tours may take a little longer, but you'll develop a much stronger relationship with the parent in comparison to any other settings that they have viewed.

9. Give them something to take away.

We all love receiving gifts. When you give something to someone, they are much more likely to do or say something positive in return, it's called the law of reciprocity.

So, at the end of the tour give the child and parent a goodie bag with an age-appropriate gift (educational or fun based), some branded merchandise and some inexpensive items like a coloring book and colors. For the parent, you could put in a small pampering gift from one of your local business partners. It's another way to set you apart from the competition and get those parents talking about you.

10. Ask for the enrollment.

This often scares a lot of people when it comes to asking for money, but you have to look at it from a different angle. If you think your setting is the right place for a child, where they'll get the best care and education, then you have a duty of care to ask for the enrollment. It's important to finish the tour by bringing them to a quiet room/area where you can ask for the enrollment. Tell the parent you think their child would blossom in the appropriate room, and you'd love to get them enrolled today. You can put their mind at ease as your setting has everything they are looking for and then discuss the pricing. This will be uncomfortable at first, but the more you practice this, the more you'll get used to it. Remember, if you think you've got the best solution for that child, you have a duty of care to ask for the enrollment.

Bonus 1. The Follow-Up

You may show parents around your setting who just simply aren't ready to enrol yet. They may have only just had their baby and are looking at their options, so having a thorough follow-up campaign is crucial to securing that enrollment.

Ideally, this needs to be an automated system that schedules reminders and sends emails for you and arranges a series of follow-up tasks.

If you'd like to take a look at a sample follow-up campaign, be sure to get our free template by visiting www.childcaretoptips.com/resources

The 'Cost' To Acquire A Customer

Jenna Williams

In this chapter, we're going to dive into the 'cost' to acquire a customer. When I say 'cost' I don't just mean a financial cost, there's a lot more to it than that. I remember when we opened our first building, we thought it would be easy to get full quickly, but we were so wrong. In this chapter, I'll break down the true cost to acquire a customer and how this can completely change your business once you start to implement it in your business.

1. Setting a marketing budget is just the start

I remember when we opened our first location, we set a rough marketing budget for each month, but Nick quickly overspent in the first few weeks alone. We had an open day planned and Nick hired mascot suits to stand out on the street promoting the open day. Don't get me wrong, it worked, but these alone blew our monthly budget. So, if you haven't already set a budget, set one and be sure to try and stick to it.

2. What does it cost to acquire a customer?

One of the biggest mistakes we learned early on, was that we had a budget in place for marketing, but we didn't actually know what marketing was working and therefore had no idea what it was costing us to acquire a customer. So, I'm going to breakdown how you can work out the actual cost of acquiring the customer.

If you have a budget of $10 a day on Facebook ads, and you receive one inquiry per day, the cost to get an inquiry is $10 per inquiry. Now we know the cost per inquiry, we now need to know how many of those inquiries convert into customers. So let's imagine that out of 10 inquiries, you get 2 new customers. Therefore, you spent $10 per inquiry x 10 = $100. Divide this by the 2 new customers, and it cost you $50 per new customer. Be sure to track exactly where the customer came from and how much it cost you to acquire that customer.

3. Don't limit yourself with your budget

Once you know the actual cost to acquire a customer, why not scale your budget accordingly to acquire the number of customers you need? You see, if I know it costs me $50 to acquire a customer, but my budget is only $300 per month, I'm limited to only acquire 6 customers per month. Once you know the actual cost to acquire the customer, you can keep reinvesting that same amount to acquire as many customers as you need. Obviously, you need to keep a close eye on this each month as the cost may fluctuate, but this is a big game changer once you understand this. If it doesn't, go back over it, or check out some of our videos on YouTube, search Childcare Business Growth.

4. Test different platforms

One thing we do with all of our done for you clients is test different platforms. For example, your child care center may be in area with lots of large multi-site competitors. They usually have big budgets to advertise on platforms like Google, so your cost to acquire an inquiry on Google may be quite high. In that scenario, another platform like Facebook, Instagram or TikTok might actually work out considerably cheaper for you. So, be sure to get someone experienced to help you test these platforms, as you may be paying much higher than you need to be to generate an inquiry.

5. What's the 'true' cost to acquire a customer?

When we first opened, we had an open day, where over 80 people turned up. We had no booking system, it was just get as many people through the door as possible. Every one of them loved the center, and they were all given an enrollment form to get started. We left that night thinking every one of them would enroll, but we were so wrong. We later came to realize that it wasn't just good enough showing parents around as part of the tour, there was a process to a successful follow-up.

I went back and tracked every one of those inquiries and 52 out of the 80 enrolled. Some took as little as the next day to bring back their paperwork, whereas some took as long as 18 months! That requires time and commitment to follow them up, and I honestly don't believe we would have gained those customers unless we were robust on our follow-up, and that's where the 'true' cost to acquire a customer comes in. Actual is how much you spend, whereas 'true' is the total amount of work involved.

6. The Follow-Up

You may show parents around your setting who just simply aren't ready to enrol yet. They may have only just had their baby and are looking at their options, so having a thorough follow-up campaign is crucial to securing that enrollment. Ideally, this needs to be an automated system that schedules reminders and sends emails for you and arranges a series of follow-up tasks.

Here's a simple example of a follow-up process.

- Send a postcard or thank you card immediately after the tour.
- Some parents will be visiting other settings, or looking to make a decision quickly. Use this to judge how quickly to follow up.
- Tell the parent you will follow up with them within two days, unless the parent has specifically told you a reason otherwise.
- If the parent doesn't answer, send them a follow-up text and email.
- Wait two days and follow up again.

For more examples, go to www.childcaretoptips.com/resources

7. Clearly define your follow-up process

If your team are going to be doing the follow-up for you, be sure to clearly define what you want them to do. How often do you want them to call? How often do you want them to text or email? I often hear people say, "If they're interested, they'll call back." People are busy, but that doesn't mean they are not interested. I remember calling one parent as part of a follow-up process, and she said, "Thank you so much for calling me back, as the other four centers I visited didn't call me back, and it made me feel like I wasn't good enough!" How terrible is it that a parent was unintentionally made to feel this way.

You're probably going to have team members that are nervous to follow up with a parent for fear of upsetting them or bothering them too much. To be honest, I felt exactly the same way for a long time, but we run a business after all and running a business involves sales. Hopefully the example I gave above of the parent not being called gives your team some inspiration on just how important it is to follow up frequently. So, be sure to stipulate to your team the exact process you want followed.

8. Take down notes and schedule tasks

When a parent attends a tour, they'll give you lots of information about themselves and their child. Some will tell you what they love about your setting in comparison to others they've been to see. All this information is so important to write down. Then, when you follow up with the parent, you can remind them of the points they raised, but they'll also be grateful of the points you remembered about them.

Another example of this is remembering to call at a particular time. We have lots of parents come for a tour, and then they'll tell us they have other settings to see, but to call the following Tuesday. Or, maybe they're going on holiday and they want us to call when they get back. You must make sure you schedule and complete that call. I know lots of people like to use a paper diary, but I personally prefer an online platform that reminds me when to call and exactly what I need to say. Now, if one of my team did the tour, and they just happen to be off today, I can still pick up the task. How great would it be if I read the notes and asked the parent how their holiday went? It's attention to detail and shows we care.

9. How to get feedback from tours

Feedback from tours is essential to better understand exactly what potential families think of your facility. For example, if a parent really likes your center, you want to get in contact with them as soon as possible to get them to sign up. Or, a parent may have a concern that they didn't feel was addressed on the tour. It's important to get that feedback as quickly as possible. Here are some ways to try and get that feedback.

- Always try to ring the parent first.

- If they don't answer, send a text, as they are far more likely to respond and be honest via a text message.

- You could send a survey link using Google Forms or Typeform where they can leave feedback anonymously. That way, they'll be more likely to be honest with you.

- Use an automated follow up system like www.childcareautomation.com that you can schedule to go out as soon as they've been for the tour.

Here's an example follow-up text you can use:

"Hi _____ I hope you don't mind me following up on your tour. I totally understand how busy you are, and you may have not yet made a decision about your childcare options, but I'd be really grateful if you could take a few minutes to give me your honest feedback on how the tour went for you, as we're always looking for ways to keep improving our service. Please be as honest as possible, as we really do value your opinion."

10. How to respond to feedback

Whether the feedback is positive or negative, it's important to reply quickly. If feedback is negative, don't be offended - this is an opportunity to learn more about how your service is perceived, and more about the parent's needs. Always thank the parent for their feedback and take onboard the points they have raised. Show how you are taking action to address any concerns. Remember, parents spend time with other parents, so if we don't address their concerns, their opinions could spread very quickly.

If you'd like to get more tips on working out the cost to acquire a customer, or how you can put in place better follow-up systems, be sure to check out our website www.childcarebusinessgrowth.com

OPERATIONS

Opening Your First Location

Joy Maxwell

At this moment, think of what has brought you to this place. Why are you here reading this book? What caused you to think about how you could help little ones and make a greater impact each day you go to work? Knowing your "why" can help you perform with passion and purpose.

In 2013, I played with the idea of opening a child care center day and night. I thought about the center's name, how I wanted it to look, how many students I wanted to attend. I thought about it ALL THE TIME. Then, in the summer of 2014, I told my principal that I would not be returning to teach the following September. I shared my idea with a few people, and, to be honest, they weren't 100 percent encouraging. However, that didn't stop me. I started gathering all the things I needed for my childcare business.

I didn't have much money starting, so I went to local flea markets, thrift stores, donation centers, and book banks to find everything I needed. When you don't have a lot of funding, you need to get creative. The hardest part for me was finding the exact space I needed to use in my house for my future business. My basement was the perfect place; it had a private bathroom and a separate entrance. However, that was my husband's man cave, and he didn't want to see it go. So, I had to go to my husband and have a very serious conversation. I told him if he allowed me to use the basement for the childcare center, we would get a 100 percent return on our investment. Now, we were making progress. That man cave was about to become my business.

1. Mindset vs Skill set

As long as you have the mindset that you will be successful in this industry, you can learn the skillset to make it happen. Your mindset is your strongest skill so make sure you keep it strong from the very beginning. If you need a little help with this, then this book is the perfect place to start. Too many people I hear from feel like they don't have the skills to operate a childcare center. They feel afraid of failing. While those feelings are valid, they should not inhibit your progress.

This is why it is imperative to work on your mindset before your skillset. The skills will come once your mindset is on track.

2. Understanding State Rules

The first and most important area I would suggest for any childcare enthusiast to start with would be to research all the regulations that apply to you and your business. I can't emphasize this point enough. It's so, so, so important. This means you need to look into your state, area, district, and jurisdiction regulations. It would be best to start with understanding and following the childcare licensing set up regulations for your local area. These regulations will be your go-to guide for the specific areas you need to consider.

Generally, these guidelines will tell you precisely what is required regarding the amount of square footage on your premises, what your child to staff ratios must be, if you need indoor or outdoor play space, and how much space you need for those sections when needed. Child care regulations are always a good start but keep in mind they are usually the bare necessities of what you will need to open your child care facility. Always ensure that you are following the correct regulations for your business.

3. It's More Than a Name. Secure It, Fast!

I have two important tips when it comes to choosing your name. The first tip is to name your child care program something that has room for growth. The second tip is making sure you register your name correctly and trademark it. When you do this, make sure you are specific with the trademark details and any other type of business that could grow from your company. All of this should be included in your application.

During the summer of 2013, I remember trying to create a name for my child care program. I had been stuck for a while when my husband walked in from work and extended his arms around me. I assumed he was coming in for his usual evening greeting, but as he got closer, he said, "I know what to call it - let's call it 'open arms.'" We embraced, just as the name described, and it just resonated in my spirit. At that moment, my first business was born, Open Arms.

When I registered my name, we made a slight mistake. We named our center for where we were at the time. We didn't think about where we might go the future. That's why the first Open Arms was called "Open Arms Family Child Care."

The name sounded good at the time. However, after one year, we moved into our group facility and closed our home program. We realized that the name no longer aligned with our mission. That's when we had to go back to the name registry bureau and apply to change our name again.

You need to make sure that you are filing your business correctly to best work for you for the long term.

It's better to get all of your questions answered by an expert before starting. Don't be intimidated about paying for information. I promise you, it will save you time, money, and heartache in the long run. Once you have chosen your name, do a quick search online to ensure that your name is not already being used. I would advise you to start the trademark process as soon as possible..

4. It's All About The Benjamins

When I first opened my child care business in 2013, a friend told me that I did not have to report business taxes as long as I didn't make over $20,000 per year. Remember, I had been a classroom teacher teaching elementary students all my life; I knew absolutely nothing about business and finances. I only knew how to love, nurture and educate children, and that's what I wanted to focus on - not all the business and finance side of things. By the end of my first full year of business, I hired a tax preparer, and I was shocked when she started asking me for specific documentation that I did not have nor had ever heard of them. There were three major financial issues that I had in my business when I first started:

- I was spending, but not counting

- I was co-mingling funding

- I had no money automation

I cleared my savings and pulled my 401(k) to start my second childcare program. That meant I was very used to spending money for my business and not documenting if the company was making enough money to support what I was spending. This is what I mean by spending and not counting.

To avoid making the same mistakes I did, you need to create a budget and stick to it. This budget has to be your bottom line. When you are strict on your budget, you will find ways to wait until more revenue comes in before making too many purchases. Remember, it's ok to start with second-hand items until you can get them first hand, and it's also ok to take donations. Outline everything you need and exactly how much you can safely allot to each item to avoid jeopardizing your bottom line.

5. Co-Mingling Funds

Number one rule of running your business - *never co-mingle your funds*. Your business and personal funds need to be separate from the word go. When I first opened my business, if I was out and saw something that the daycare required, I would purchase it without thinking. It didn't matter if I used my personal debit card or my business card. Then, when I realized my personal funds were dwindling, I would use my business account to cover some personal expenses - hoping that everything would balance out.

This is an accounting nightmare. Don't make this mistake. Keep everything separate so that you can navigate your funds with ease.

6. Finding The Right Location

An old saying goes: "in business, location is everything."

To date, I've opened five businesses in 6 different locations, and I can safely say that the saying is true.

Our first location was in our home, and although we did pretty good with word-of-mouth clients, we didn't do well with clients from the neighborhood. After a month of being open and talking to my neighbors, I realized that there was a free Pre/k program directly behind my house in the basement of the local elementary school.

If I had done a location analysis I would have known to focus on the toddlers and infants because the neighborhood had the preschoolers taken care of.

Now when I secure buildings, I always ask about :

- Zoning
- Square footage
- Lease type

- Lease duration

- Deposit requirements

- If it has been a child care facility in the past

- If there is a grace period for collected rent after the lease has been signed

The above questions have saved me a *lot* of time and money. I'm sure they will save you too.

Once I ask all these questions during a viewing, I tend to spend some time in the neighborhood. I walk or drive around, looking for good signs in the neighborhood. For example, I look out for areas with children's bikes, trampolines, basketball nets, play equipment, chalk writings, or drawings on the sidewalk and walls.

Next, I go to the US census website and see how many households have children in the area.

From that point, I go and visit the neighborhood schools.

With all this information, you are better equipped to make the right decision about your location and the future of your business. It takes some time. However, it will make it worth it in the end.

7. Marketing The Successful Way

As soon as you have legally secured your business name, go and register for a TikTok, Snapchat, Facebook, and Instagram. All of these platforms are considered free marketing real estate, and you should have a presence on all platforms to make sure you are reaching as many people as possible. Please take advantage of these platforms, use them frequently, and engage with your followers.

When parents research where they will choose for their child, it doesn't look good if your page has been inactive for months. They'll be wondering if your business still exists

Be active. Be present. These platforms are free for you to use. Using them correctly will start making you money instead of wasting it on other forms of advertising to your target market.

If you need help with creating these things, you can go to any freelance website and outsource some help. Go on Fiver and find an expert to create templates for you, set up your pages, or create a childcare start-up budget template. Your business doesn't need to be entirely done by you. Ask for help in the areas you are not familiar with yet - it will make your life so much easier!

8. Gather Your Supplies, Create Your Policies

When you have your startup list created and your location secured, I suggest you go into your space and start to visualize where you want to place everything in your center. This is so much easier when you know how much room you are working with and how it is laid out.

Create a vision board for your classroom. On it, you should include pictures of furniture you'd like, bookshelves, toys, chairs, tables, and all other supplies you'd like to have for your center.

Everything you can imagine, you should put in your vision board and plan where it will go. When it comes to purchasing items, don't overstretch your budget if you don't have that much to work with just yet.

Once you have a plan in place for the layout of your business, it's time to do some paperwork. Creating policies, practices, and procedures is essential for the success of your childcare business.

You can look up how other businesses structure their policies to see how they can fit your idea of doing business. Once you have an outline of your policies and procedures, you need to think about how you will make sure that they are adhered to throughout your business.

The more thought and structure you put into that now, the easier it will be when you have staff. It will create an accessible overview of what you expect and how things should be done, even when you are not in the building to supervise. It sets an expectation that you want everyone to live up to.

This professionalism will shine throughout your business when you set a firm foundation to build from.

9. Provide Top Quality Care

Congratulations, you've made it!

You have:

- A name and a location
- Read the regulations
- Consulted with a child care coach Created the best policies, practices, and procedures Set up your social media accounts
- Designed your location
- Gathered the supplies

Now, it's time to open your doors for business!

Starting your services with quality and maintaining high quality is the challenging part of doing business. However, I know you are up for the challenge!

What I've learned is not only do you want to strive always to be operating a quality program, but you also want to document that you're running a quality program in line with local regulations. If you start to cut corners, it will show. Worst case scenario, you will get shut down until you comply. This leads to wasted money and frustrated parents. Believe me, that is not good for business.

10. Get Feedback and Keep Improving!

When your business is doing well, make sure you try to prove that. Ask families to leave a review for you online. This can be on Google, your social media pages, or otherwise. You can even make posts about it on your social media pages with a quote from a parent that advocates for your quality business.

Parents trust other parents' opinions and reviews are the easiest way to prove you are the service they need!

There You Have It. Thank you so much for reading this chapter. I'm so glad you took this step for your future business. Preparation is key to your success.

I hope you take all you've learned today and work it into the best plan for your quality business. Remember, don't cut any corners. It may seem like a shortcut when you're starting a business, but it will come back to bite you later. Think every step through, budget well, and plan accordingly. That's your recipe for success!

Until next time, you got this!

Bonus Business Checklist

- Name research
- Name registration
- Trademark application
- Business registration
- Business bank account
- Regulation research
- Print all documents
- Location planning
- Location selection
- Supply planning
- Supply purchasing
- Marketing plan
- Social media plan
- Open doors
- SUCCEED!

With nearly 15 years of experience in childcare, Joy is the inspirational mindset coach you have been searching for!

After working as a teacher's aid, a spark was lit inside Joy, driving her in her journey to becoming a teacher and educating young children. Joy earned her Masters in Early Childcare Education and Multicultural Education at Eastern University and uses her knowledge and understanding of education to inspire others.

You can find out more about working with Joy by visiting: https://vip.thejoyof-childcare.com/

Operational Strategies

Summer Picha

Have you ever been to the circus and watched the plate spinners? The art of balance, concentration, and entertainment draws viewers, holds their attention potentially waiting for a slip up. Running a childcare business can feel much like being a plate spinner in the circus. When you are plate spinning you have several activities (that require your total attention) happening at the same time rather than focusing on one single project at a time.

Keeping those plates spinning is the nature of our business.

To lessen the intensity of the spinning plates we need to talk about organizing operations in your program. Before we can dive into the "how" we must first define what operations mean. A definition of operations that our program came up with was "The ability to carry out the activities involved in the day to day functions of the business so that the school can continue to provide quality care and generate profits." Now, this is the definition that we used in our program, you are welcome to use it if it fits what you do. However, I highly encourage you to take some time to think about what the definition of operations that fits your program is. Next, solidify it by talking about operations as a leadership team, writing it down, and incorporating it into the culture of your program.

Now that everyone is on the same page about "what" operations are it's time to dive into the "how" to organize the operations in your program so you can deliver the best quality care for the children in your program. Let's start by looking at the top ten tips to organize your operations.

1. Organizational Chart

Who does what when? AND how do your staff know who to go to when they have a particular need. This is where an organizational chart come into play. Most organizational charts include the hierarchy; owner, director, administrator, teacher, support staff and so on. To have massive success in your program I am going to encourage you to take your chart one step further. Include the staff member, title, how to contact, and responsibilities. If the owner is responsible for all financial decisions let your team know that they should be talking to the owner about getting that raise! If the director is a whiz at licensing rules and regulations instruct your staff to chat with the director about compliance questions. A simple question about turning in accident reports, the administrative assistant can help with that.

This new organizational chart doesn't just appear out of thin air, it is imperative that you and your leadership team have honest conversations about skill sets, roles, and expectations. By simply adding contact information and role responsibilities you are setting your staff up for success.

2. Licensing and Compliance

As childcare leaders we know compliance is crucial to running a quality program. Having a checks and balance system in place to ensure all staff know, understand and follow licensing guidelines is imperative. What does licensing and compliance management mean to your organization? How can you ensure that your staff are following all licensing guidelines? Ongoing training opportunities, quality control observations by the leadership team, and monthly 1:1 staff meetings will ensure compliance and help you, as the leader, sleep at night.

3. Handbook vs. Training Manual

Do you know the difference between the employee handbook and the training manual? I always tell my leadership team that the handbook is full of legal "stuff" that the lawyer requires you to tell your employees. It is important to have legal counsel review your handbook annually to make sure it is current as well as compliant with any new laws. The training manual on the other hand is a step-by-step guide on HOW to complete all tasks in your program. The idea of breaking down everything in your program may feel overwhelming (sidenote: it WILL feel overwhelming). Once you decide on a format for your training manual divide and assign the tasks into bite size pieces with the end goal of completing the training manual in 12 months.

4. Building Maintenance

A part of the job that many leaders overlook until they are in it is facilities management. I suggest pulling out a calendar and recording tasks by month. For example tasks such as fire extinguisher renewals, sprinkler maintenance, lawn care, and snow removal can be scheduled in advance and anticipated annually. Organizing the anticipated maintenance will free up time for the unexpected challenges that arise, hello leaky roof!

5. Employee Recruitment and Retention

Our business is people working with people. Without quality staff the program would be nothing. From interviewing to training and everything in between the ability to create, implement, and review employee skill development is important for the success of our program.

6. Staff Management

Finding and hiring staff isn't the finish line with it comes to staff. Childcare leaders are responsible for daily communication with employees. Tasks include providing a schedule, ongoing training, performance reviews, conflict resolution, relationship building, payroll and much more. Continuing to build your leadership skills in staff management will largely improve how your program is run and staff morale.

7. Customer Service

The childcare industry is a people-oriented field. Staff, children, and parents make up our entire world. I always say, "the children are our jobs, the parents are our customers." What is your vision of customer service in your program, how are you training your staff to uphold the vision? Every interaction with parents can be looked at through the lens of customer service. Does your facility smell good? Is there someone to greet them when they enter? Is these a policy on wiping the child's face before the parents arrive?

8. Childcare

It seems obvious to include childcare under the operations section. However, putting into words the expectations of what childcare means helps your team understand the job. The definition of childcare that I used in my program is the ability to supervise and nurture children so the children are safe, their basic human needs are met, and they are progressing emotionally, socially, academically and physically. What does childcare mean to you and your team?

9. Financial Management

Financial Management speaks to the ability to send and receive payments, monitor monetary resources, and plan for future financial needs so your program can continue to operate and the longevity of the business is not compromised. Even if looking at your financials is not your favorite task begin to develop good money habits by scheduling monthly financial meetings in addition to annual budget strategy sessions with your accountant. Financial health ensures a healthy long term program.

10. Business Development

Business development is the ability to grow in size as well as quality. Annual strategic planning sessions with your leadership team will ensure that management is striving for the same big goals to develop the program. Once you have your annual strategy session your responsibility as the owner or founder is to set up and monitor quarterly goals for your leadership team. These short term goals help your management support the big goal. Breaking it down even further, monthly leadership meetings to monitor progress and even weekly check in's to keep your finger on the pulse of your business.

Setting up meetings to check in with your leadership team keeps everyone on task and working towards the betterment of your business. At the end of the day, your business won't run itself—it takes time and attention to create a quality program that you will be proud of!

Summer Picha is a Minneapolis / Twin Cities-based early childhood development and leadership expert who helps early childhood programs, schools and facilities become the best-in-class choice for their clients and customers and be an integrated part of raising good humans.

She's the creator of the Conscious Classroom Certification Model: the leading framework that helps owners and administrators retain staff, recruit families, reduce risk by staying compliant without complication, and protect school revenue while running a fast-paced facility in ever-changing times.

Leveraging Summer's 18+ years in the industry and her role as co-founder of a group of award-winning and highly-referred Montessori schools in the Twin Cities, Summer knows specifically what it takes to lead a mission-driven team and create a culture where schools and families feel like they belong.

Operational Excellence in Child Care through Best Practice and Compliance

Martin Bing

We will explore what Operational Excellence looks like and explore the importance of creating systems, processes, and procedures. Together we will consider ways to manage and monitor operational excellence.

Let's dig in.

Today, Maria is helping clean up after naptime in the toddler classroom. She doesn't normally work in this room, but is happy to fill in when needed. Maria thought she could simplify the process of clean up by storing the labeled cot sheets and blankets directly on each child's designated cot. She thought this would not only keep the nap materials organized, but save them time, making it easy to locate the correct cot and bedding for each child tomorrow. She felt good about the way things were organized and was proud of how quickly she finished the task.

The next day Debbie began getting the room ready for naptime and soon became frustrated because she couldn't easily find what she needed. Normally, she would retrieve the blankets and sheets from each child's individual cubby when setting up the nap cots. But today she found everything stored together. Some children that were here yesterday aren't here today, and other part-time children filled in. Because their normal process wasn't followed, Debbie had to spend extra time figuring out which cots were ready to go and which still needed to be sanitized and set up.

Maria and Debbie BOTH had systems for the cleanup of naptime materials. Each of their systems accomplished the goals of organization and storage, and neither one of them was "wrong." The problem was that their systems were DIFFERENT. They weren't clearly communicated or agreed upon, and it cost them each some time and frustration as staff had to adapt to figure out how to accomplish their tasks.

The more in sync your team can become, the closer they will get to truly operating in excellence. This chapter is dedicated to helping you stop small operational inefficiencies like this *(and compounded if you are a larger center or multisite)* that could keep you from reaching your full potential.

We will explore what Operational Excellence looks like, how you can create systems, processes, and procedures for your school, and implement required checklists to keep your team accountable to your brand standards. We will also take a look at how you can measure and analyze data from your compliance reports and use that information to improve your business. After all, the better your business functions, the bigger of an impact you can make in the lives of the children and families you serve.

1. Operational Excellence Redefined in Early Education

Operational Excellence is not a common term in childcare, but it should be. The idea of continually striving to improve resonates with most child care business owners. We all want to provide the best we can for the families in our care. If you are a child care leader, whether you represent an in-home program, a licensed center, multisite brand, franchisees, or franchisors, now is the time to step up to the plate and set an example for others to follow.

We realize that every business is on a different path, but no matter where you are in your journey, you can take steps to impact best practice in our industry.

Let's first define excellence and discuss its first cousin, best in class. *Excellence* is simply the quality of being outstanding or extremely good. *Best in Class* typically refers to a company that has set the benchmark that others in the industry seek to at least meet in order to be competitive, although the goal is often to exceed that mark and set a new industry standard.

When you strive for excellence in every aspect of your school, it really matters. Your culture of excellence will show in everything you do, from your curb sign to how tidy your lobby is kept. From your classroom organization, to your playground maintenance and safety.

Are your bathrooms as clean as your kitchens?

Let's get away from the idea that "good enough" is enough. Let's exceed expectations and set the benchmark for excellence.

2. Systems, Processes and Procedures…. Lions Tigers and Bears, Oh MY!

If you don't already have well documented processes and procedures, it might feel a bit overwhelming to get started with creating systems for your child care business. However, it really is simpler than you think. Chances are you already have a repeatable "way of doing things." The key is to just get started by writing down all the steps involved, so you will be able to communicate your systems to your team.

Creating systems will allow you to replicate your processes, so your families experience the same level of high-quality service no matter which employee they interact with. This is achieved because each new employee is trained to do things according to your system and they understand what is expected to meet standards and ensure compliance. Even when an employee knows every step of every process, memory occasionally fails and interruptions happen, so it's important to have a standard to measure compliance against.

Begin by creating a list of tasks or activities that you or your team does on a daily, weekly, or monthly basis. Start with the most common things such as preparing the room for naptime, creating a lesson plan, or shutting down a classroom at the end of the day.

Next, choose one of the tasks and begin to flesh out instructions. Think about supplies or resources that might be needed, where things are kept, and the order in which things need to be completed. If possible, ask a team member to read through what you've written to see if they can think of anything you've missed. Brainstorm for solutions if you discover any gaps.

3. Checklists – They are Vital to Operational Best Practice and Excellence

It can take 13 years after high school graduation to become a surgeon. Woah, that's a ton of schooling, training, practice, and supervision. I think it's safe to say that by the time they are ready to practice on their own, surgeons are pretty much experts in their field. They *know* what they are doing.

Yet, despite this expert level of knowledge and experience, you'd be hard-pressed to find a surgeon who would even set foot in an operating room without first consulting their checklist. This is because surgeons (and many other professionals) know the power of the checklist when it comes to quality, safety, compliance, and operational excellence.

In his book the *Checklist Manifesto*, Atul Gawande explores the importance of using simple checklists when working through both simple and complex processes. He studied several professions and cites many examples of improvements in the medical field. For example, *when the state of Michigan began using a checklist for central lines in its intensive care units, in just 3 months its infection rate dropped 66%. Soon, its ICUs were outperforming 90% of all hospitals nationwide. In 18 months, the checklist saved an estimated 175 million dollars and 1500 lives.*

Checklists are not an option; they are essential when creating best practices and operating in excellence. They save time, reduce error, keep you focused, ensure consistency, improve productivity, help ensure compliance, and more.

Checklists help you stay focused, since the important steps are clearly spelled out. They will help you ensure that the important stuff gets done - and done the right way. Not only is it easy to forget a step once in a while, but sometimes people veer off course, thinking they know a "better way" to get it done. Eliminate variations and inconsistencies in quality by agreeing on and following your process checklists.

If hospitals that use checklists for operations have experienced overall drops in their death rates of thirty to fifty percent, imagine the improvements you can make in your early learning program.

Not only can you improve the productivity of your team, the cleanliness of your facilities, and the safety of your program, but you can truly impact the lifelong outcomes of so many children by following checklists in your child care center. Studies show that children with quality early education experiences achieve higher levels of education, earn larger salaries, have fewer health issues, and more fulfilling relationships.

To uplevel your childcare business, take your processes and procedures and create checklists from them. Communicate the requirements for completing them with your team in a way that highlights your WHY for serving children. Remind them of the difference you make and the mission you are on together. Get the team bought in to operational excellence and continuous improvement, and then hold them accountable to the new way of doing things.

4. Audit – What You Don't Know, CAN Hurt You

In a recent survey of child care business owners, 52% reported hanging a check-list clipboard in their classrooms as a reminder to their staff of what to do. These owners WANT their team to follow their processes and procedures, and while a few did have a system in place for monitoring this, nearly two-thirds of respondents admitted that they haven't put any checks or balances into place to ensure that their expectations are actually being followed.

Imagine thinking your team is golden. They know the regulations and requirements. They know what's expected of them on a daily basis. But inevitably they miss a major safety issue resulting in a violation - or worse yet, an injury to a child – all because routine audits on checklist completion were not being conducted. In a large percentage of cases, this could have been avoided.

A common mantra in business states, *"You must inspect what you expect."* Placing a high level of importance on completing the checklists and holding your team accountable by checking their work will result in a much higher level of compliance. It's clear that no matter the size of your business, you need a system for monitoring your expectations so your center can truly operate in excellence.

5. Measurement and Refinement

So far we've established that running a center of excellence requires well documented processes and procedures, checklists for the team to remind them of important and required tasks, and a system of monitoring compliance with your established checklists. If you get all of this in place, you are well on your way to the operational excellence you imagine.

But there's more you can do to ensure quality and compliance when you begin to measure the data from your checklists. Many providers might not even realize that there is data that can be measured and analyzed from cleaning check-lists, classroom compliance checks, injury reports, and maintenance records.

Up until this point in this chapter, all the actions detailed could be completed on your own, without the aid of a special tool or software. However, analyzing a binder full of checklists is never going to give you the information and data that a digital solution can because when it comes to measuring data, it is difficult to organize and pull this information from several assorted paper records. Luckily, when you begin using a digital tool, such as 1Place Childcare software, the digital dashboards of compiled data will allow you to not only confirm compliance, but identify trends, make decisions or improvements, and spot any gaps that might exist - whether you're in the center/s or remote. You'll gain answers and insights into your business that you never knew you needed.

Measuring your checklist compliance data can do so much to help you improve your business practices.

6. The Value of Reporting

A picture is worth a thousand words, it's true. The visual nature of a snapshot can often tell us more with a quick glance than several paragraphs of detailed descriptive words.

In business, reporting tools can give us that quick snapshot as to how our business is doing. At a glance, you can see in visual form exactly where you stand on any given measurable.

Management theorist, Peter Drucker, said, *"What gets measured gets improved."* Karl Pearson expanded on that to say, *"That which is measured and reported improves exponentially."*

Unless you measure something and regularly monitor your reports, you won't know if it is getting better or worse. You will not be able to see positive progress or identify complacency. The trick is to understand the value of data and measure the right things. How valuable would it be to get a single comprehensive view into your business operations so you could make informed decisions?

Whether it's your board of directors, your investors, the families you serve, your staff, your community, or the children in your care, everybody benefits from increased accountability. Begin by measuring your operational compliance data, running reports, and making adjustments and improvements when your results indicate the need. Soon your reports will serve as proof to your stakeholders that you run a center of excellence.

MEASURE - REPORT - IMPROVE
Digital Reporting Gives You a Visual Snapshot of Operational Excellence

Compliance Completion

At a glance, view completion of licensing criteria across all centers, to ensure best practice standards are being met.

Classroom Management

Track metrics across educators and staff to manage key aspects such as attitude, iniative, professionalism, and professional development.

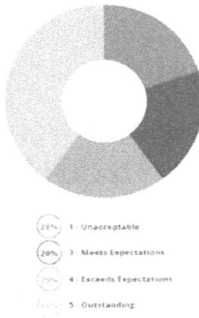

Active Supervision Comparison

Quickly identify gaps and successes - so you can proactively put measures in place.

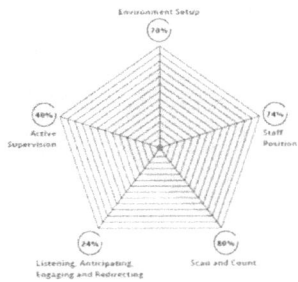

1Place
Childcare
COMPLIANCE & BEST PRACTICE MADE EASY

7. The Value of Operational Compliance Data vs Information vs Knowledge vs Wisdom

Ok, Great! Now you have a ton of operational compliance data. The question is, what do you do with it?

The goal is to take the data (*did it happen or not?*) and turn that into information by analyzing how well or how poorly it happened.

For instance, imagine your preschool teachers are taking the children to the playground. Let's look at how well they followed your safety process. Did they begin applying sunscreen 20 minutes before heading outside? Did they check

116

diapers and take the potty-trainers to the restroom? Did they ensure the classroom centers were cleaned up and their room was tour ready? Did they gather all the water bottles to bring with them? Did they perform their name to face checks, ensuring every child is accounted for? You get the idea.

Once you have the knowledge gained from the information about how well your process was completed against your brand standard or best practice, you can apply wisdom to identify how you can improve or refine your process. You might determine that you need to tweak your process by adding an additional aide to the class to help prepare for playground time, or by keeping a water cooler and paper cups on the playground to simplify the process of taking the children outside.

8. Operational Excellence is Not a Destination

When striving for excellence, it's important to remember that you'll never actually arrive at your destination. There will always be something more you can do to make your business better. What works well today may change later when a new technology is developed or a new licensing regulation is announced. Embrace the fact that you are on a journey and your route may change many times.

Operating using best practices is a practice in itself. Getting honest with yourself and your data, so you know what is working and what isn't takes courage. It is an indicator of your commitment to continual improvement.

9. Your Leadership Shadow - A Reflection of You

As an owner, or a leader of your organization, the way your business operates is truly a reflection of you. What type of shadow are you casting?

It doesn't matter what your title is. The fact is you're leading your team in some capacity, and being a leader implies that people are following you. Everything that happens in your business is a direct result of something that you've said, modeled, or tolerated. YOU set the tone for the culture of your school and how you accomplish your mission. What you care about, your staff will care about.

Since your team is following in your shadow, be sure you are leading them to a place of excellence and growth. Define your systems and processes, implement best practices, require checklists, measure data, make informed decisions, and stay on the path of continual improvement. Be sure your legacy makes a difference for generations to come by operating in excellence today.

10. Impact – Remember Why

We've spent a lot of time discussing some of the not-so-glamorous aspects of running a child care business: systems, checklists, and operational compliance. It might feel like these are things that "just need to get done" and don't really make an impact, but they do. Just because something doesn't evoke emotion, doesn't mean it doesn't make a difference that can be deeply felt.

- What would happen if allergy checks weren't completed and a child went into anaphylactic shock?

- How would your school recover if a child was left on the playground or in a van?

- Do you think you might attract more families if curb appeal and tour-ready checklists were regularly completed? What would extra revenue mean for your business?

- Would achieving an accreditation status increase demand for your center? Would it improve the quality of education, impacting the children's educational futures?

- How would it impact the families you serve, and your community as a whole, if your center were shut down due to an avoidable licensing violation?

As you can see, improving your processes and continually striving for operational excellence makes a huge impact.

We hope that you can see the value of establishing and monitoring your operational processes and are inspired to either get started or make improvements to what you have in place. Remember your WHY and your mission, and try to include little glimpses of it into what you create.

Martin Bing, Founder & CEO of 1Place Childcare

Martin Bing has over 20 years of experience in technology and entrepreneurial companies. It was in 2006 when Martin identified a need for an online tool that multisite and franchise organizations could use to measure consistency and share information.

The resulting software – based on digitized checklists – was named 1Place and was soon helping childcare and fast-food franchises manage compliance across their various sites, providing visibility for head office management and franchisors to monitor their department and franchisee operations.

Today, 1Place has found a niche servicing multi-site businesses in childcare, retail, hospitality, health and aged care industries.

As legislation tightens rules around compliance and monitoring, Martin believes the ever-growing multi-site and multi-department market requires 1Place now more than ever.

Ultimately, Martin sees 1Place as a tool for good, that not only benefits their customers but creates redemptive spaces for the wider community.

Want to Learn More?

Place Childcare is a digital compliance management platform, purpose-built for the Early Childhood sector. Whether you are a single center or a group of many, 1Place lets you standardize your processes and make best practice your business-as-usual.

How does it work?

Our secure, cloud-based app lets your team log all required day-to-day checklists and incidents, via tablet or smartphone.

Maintenance tickets can be raised, and photos taken and uploaded directly within the app, keeping details of all your safety actions and tasks in one place.

From here, our smart dashboards bring essential information to your fingertips – allowing you to analyze and improve performance, either on site or remotely.

Contact Us:

For more information contact hello@1Placeonline.com or visit www.1PlaceChildcare.com

Automate Your Business

Debbie Lawson

As any child care owner or director knows, you can quickly get lost in the day-to-day tasks in the setting, you can be called to cover in the ratios or during the busy lunchtimes, leaving your administrative tasks till you 'get time.' In the 10 points below, I will aim to show you how automating some of these tasks can buy back your time, so you can focus more on the tasks you enjoy.

These 10 are by no means the only uses of automations, but from experience these are the most useful we have set up and used over the years.

1. Inquiry follow-ups

Using a system of automated emails and SMS messages can help keep your child care setting in the forefront of your new prospective parents minds. Busy center directors may not have the time to focus their attention on all the new inquiries coming into your center, so setting up a sequence of emails and SMS messages can help keep the inquiry alive. A good CRM system such as www.childcareautomation.com can automate this process for you. An inquiry entered on your website can be added to your email sequence starting the conversation with the prospect parent. Adding SMS messages had been proven to improve the conversion of the inquiry to a paying parent, as busy parents tend to respond a lot more over SMS than email, but that doesn't mean don't use emails.

2. Tour bookings

Now your automated follow ups are working, you need to ensure the inquirer turns up for their tour. Using emails and SMS sending reminders 24 hours before, including maps and any special notes about accessing your site will help a higher show up rate for your tours, also sending thank you emails and possibly feedback questions after the tour show you care about what they thought. In www.childcareautomation.com you can combine these automations with using the built-in Calendar, so you can ensure you're not double booking or clashing with other events in your setting.

3. Sign-Ups

You now need a seamless system to get your new parents enrolled in your setting. Automating the sending out of your booking forms and enrollment packs can reduce office time for your team. You can also set up online forms, which not only capture all the information you require but can also be signed, along with adding images of ID, making the whole process much quicker for you and the parent.

4. Parent Enrichment

Using the data you've collected you can keep the personal touch with your parents automatically, such as a lovely Birthday email with a video message or SMS message from your team, or send out regular emails to keep your parents informed of events happening in your setting. If you need to send a notification of a case of Chicken Pox, use an automation to send an Email and an SMS without the team having to spend hours sending individual messages.

5. Team Recruitment

As with your inquiries, recruitment processes can be automated with applicants applying via your website, collecting CVs and asking further screening questions before you get to the actual interview stage. By using surveys and video screening software, you can save a huge amount of time and vet the candidate to an even greater depth before inviting them for an interview. How many times have you thought someone looks good on paper, but then you interview them and they just don't have the personality you're looking for. Well, using this process will help eliminate all that time-wasting and ensure you only speak to the candidates that fit your culture.

6. Team Onboarding

Giving all the team the same experience is important as new team members come aboard. Why not build out a whole team area with all the information, processes and details they need to be successful in their roles without you needing to lose yourself or another team member for multiple hours when you're not even guaranteed that the employee is going to stick around. Using a membership/training area you can build in self-tests to ensure you know they are taking in the training. Set them questions based on the documents they've read or the videos they watched. If they are not getting them correct, the system can notify you, so you can address the issues. Of course, you'll still need face to face training, but recording a lot of the content ahead of time will save you hours of work for future staff onboarding.

If you run competitions for team member of the month or similar competitions, this can go out automatically each month, send out the reminders for votes and collate the votes for you. The possibilities can be endless.

7. Overall communications

Telephone calls, SMS messages, GMB messages and Facebook Messages can all arrive at various times during the day or even out of office hours, and trying to keep on top of all those different platforms can be difficult. Using a system such as www.childcareautomation.com you can bring all the communication into one channel and respond from one central place. You can automate replies, or even send notifications to your team about any updates or communications from parents.

8. Templates

Any regular emails, letters, or general communications you send can all be made into templates and used to help cut down on administrative time. How many times have you written that same email over and over again? A well setup template will not only save you a huge amount of time, it will ensure your messaging is consistent regardless of which team member is sending the message.

9. Collecting referrals and reviews

We all know the best form of advertising is word of mouth. So, incentivize your parents to refer other parents to you. Using an automated system, you can get them to leave reviews and also refer other parents to you. You can give them their own link to track their referrals, along with thanking them and rewarding them with a great incentive scheme.

Sites like Google Business Profile love your reviews. Use automated emails or SMS with the link to your online profiles, so parents can add their reviews. Offer your parents a gift or similar if they leave you a couple of reviews on different platforms and then use an automation to thank them.

10. Fee Chasing

Chasing overdue fees can be one of the most time-consuming jobs for some businesses. Template your reminders to cut down the admin time spent on these tasks. These emails can be scheduled to go out with your timescales for chasing. For example, send a reminder on day 1 and day 4, then a stronger reminder on day 8 and 12. You can even include links to invoices where they can pay online and then the reminders stop automatically. Experience of using this type of automation has improved payments for many sites, especially the first couple of reminders, as we all know, parents are busy and sometimes forget to pay on time.

Conclusion

Any process that follows a pattern in some way can have automated elements. Take time to sit back and think about your processes and maybe with a little tweak here and there, it can become automated and save you a huge amount of time in the future.

****

Debbie Lawson is Head of Automations at Child Care Business Growth. Debbie works very closely with the team and clients building out new automations to help streamline their businesses.

If you are interested in automations or a demo, please visit of www.ChildcareAutomation.com

The Right Gears Make A Difference

Samantha Phillips

Have you ever thought about the many different components you depend on to run efficiently every day just to keep your business operating smoothly? When I think about it, I visualize mechanical gears and how the teeth of each gear fit into those around it. Like these pictured here, mechanical gears are commonly used in high load situations. Seems rather fitting since it does not get much more "high load" than owning a childcare business!

Think about it though. All the gears of your operation either work harmoniously in sync with one another in a state of constant motion, or they don't. If one rusty gear can have a detrimental impact on all the others, then making sure you have well-oiled mechanics in place is vital not only to the growth and longevity of your program, but also to your freedom and well-being.

So, what do your mechanics look like and where is there room for improvement? Below, I will share 10 areas where a professional employer organization (PEO) could make your life easier by replacing a few of those rusty worn-out gears. These changes can get your business working in unison, so you can spend less time burdened by the day-to-day mess and more time having the experiences you hoped to one day have the freedom and flexibility to enjoy as an entrepreneur.

1. Stop Handling HR

As an employer, there are federal laws that you risk accidentally violating when you don't know what you don't know. Unemployment insurance, FMLA, HIPAA, ADA, wage and hour claims, are all topics that a Certified HR professional should guide you through. "Certified" is the key word. Credentials should be verified through the issuing organization's website proving an individual has met all training requirements to be legally advising you on such highly regulated topics. Forfeit the idea of handling HR in-house (unless you have a certified team member) and enjoy the peace of mind that follows leaving it in the hands of a professional.

2. Say Goodbye to Audits

PEO's can manage many different benefits and administrative tasks that are normally managed internally. Examples of these are health care audits, work comp audits, and 401k audits. You, as the employer, not only get the benefit of large group plans that help reduce overall costs, but you also don't have to deal with stressful things like enrollments, terminations, contributions, billings, and audits anymore. Talk about a weight lifted off your shoulders!

3. Be Selective About Your Insurance Agent

Most agents are generalists, so regardless of industry, they will sell you a standard business owner's policy (BOP). There are a lot of exclusions on a standard BOP that render childcare owners completely unprotected. If the agent you are working with doesn't know what endorsements to add or exclusions to be cautioned by, you are putting yourself in a "you get what you get and don't throw a fit" situation. It is imperative to find a trustworthy childcare insurance partner. Search within your network and ask for recommendations. What "specialist" do other owners work with and why should you trust them?

4. Consolidate Your Systems

How many different platforms are you using and constantly having to monitor? One for payroll, one for staff management, one for taxes, one for childcare, one for video cameras, and potentially more? A PEO service lessens the amount of time you spend in crossing items off your to-do list each day by consolidating several of what are currently separate platforms into one single system. This move easily uncomplicates your life allowing you to focus time and energy on more pressing projects.

5. Don't Assume You Can't Afford Benefits

Employee Benefits is often an afterthought to childcare owners because most assume the cost is beyond reason. You won't be free to work outside your business until you're staffed to the point that you aren't covering a classroom anymore. This is our industry's biggest struggle right now. Offering benefits should be an integral part of your planning strategy for attracting and retaining a strong workforce. Working with a qualified Licensed Employee Benefits Broker can help you devise a cost-effective strategy of desirable health perks to help you attract those much-needed candidates.

6. Optimized Efficiencies

Working with PEO's can create integrations for the software you love and don't want to part with. Timekeeping, for instance, may be tracked by childcare management software but processed in QuickBooks. PEO's have the ability to import data, so information doesn't have to be manually input before it can be processed. They can also create custom exports for accounting systems to reduce input time and increase accuracy, because manual entry is no longer required.

7. Life Insurance is a Must

If something were to happen to you, how does your business survive? Or, maybe you have a key employee (director) that is such an integral part of your business that it would cost you substantial time and money to find a suitable replacement if they were not here anymore? A smart business owner plans for the unexpected. These are the uncomfortable circumstances for which Executive Life Insurance Policies were created. Executive Life plans should be a part of your planning strategy to ensure that your business will carry on with minimal negative impact during a crisis.

8. Tax Guarantee

Tax laws are complex and cumbersome, and the IRS is scary! They are not the organization you want catching an accidental error. Working with a qualified

PEO can make all things tax-related a painless process. Their tax software engines can identify all payroll taxes based on location and employment type. This helps remove your worry of being out of compliance with local, state, and federal laws. Some PEO's even offer a guarantee that tax payments will be made accurately and in a timely manner which eliminates your chances of paying late fees and penalties.

9. Digitize the Employee Life Cycle

Human capital management (HCM) software allows you to evolve with the future of work through state-of-the-art automation that supports a wide range of HR related functions. From recruitment, onboarding, time and attendance, payroll, benefits enrollment, expense reimbursement, and more, a secure and intuitive HCM platform capable of centralizing workplace management that is also adept to handle the above average turnover in childcare will increase your efficiency and allow you to gain back a little pre-COVID sanity.

10. Experienced Guidance

PEO's can specialize in industries like childcare to provide expert guidance on situations unique to our industry. The greatest benefit to having specialists in your corner is they know what they're talking about, because they have seen it before. Having access to someone with more specialized experience that you can call up at your convenience and bounce ideas off can help you dodge landmines others in our industry were not so fortunate to avoid. You would get assistance with decision making that before you didn't have, or that you would have had to pay consulting fees to receive.

Samantha (Sam) Phillips is a Texas native and preferred vendor with a sparkly reputation as our industry's leading expert about childcare insurance. She has helped child development centers, franchisees, private preschools, in-home, and after school programs all over the United States implement and maintain first class protection plans through her comprehensive coverage analysis and insurance partners with specialty programs for childcare businesses.

After years of serving childcare owners and learning that most of them had just trusted their insurance agent to know what coverage their business needed, Sam made it her mission to share the knowledge she spent years acquiring to help owners like you become educated consumers. Since then, her niche focus has rendered her a valuable educational resource. She's been interviewed on podcasts, guest featured on webinars, authored newsletter articles, taught lunch n learn sessions, partnered with state associations, and more, while fulfilling that mission of educating the ECE community.

Sam is now the Insurance Program Manager at Comploy, a professional employer organization and human capital management company, that streamlines back office needs not only in insurance, but also payroll, benefits, HR, and so much more. She continues rescuing owners from bad policies and sharing her expertise from a company that has a lot more to offer than just great child care insurance coverage.

Author website link: www.comployhr.com

STAFFING & DELIVERY

Staff Recruitment

Nick Williams

At the time of writing this chapter, staff recruitment is probably the hardest it's been for a long time. There is a huge shortage of qualified staff following the pandemic, and it's having a huge impact on the operations of child care facilities all over the World.

In this chapter, I'm going to share with you 10 top tips that are working for our clients right now. Be sure to take the time and check your business off against these to see if you have them all in place.

1. Don't do the same as everyone else

The problem right now is that most people are doing the same as everyone else, but expecting to get different results. You can pretty much guarantee that a lot of your competitors are also trying to recruit, but no one is actually standing out from the competition, because all the job advertisements and benefits are just the same. Start to think about every single part of the recruitment process right from the start, and challenge yourself to come up with something different to everyone else. Raise your hand as high as you can and stretch that bit further.

2. Your Values and Ethos are More Important than ever

Millennials want to feel a part of something with a bigger purpose. So, is this being portrayed in your recruitment strategy? Are your vision, mission, values and ethos all in place? Would they stand out from the crowd and attract someone to want to work for your business? Take the time to get these in place and be sure to include them on all your recruitment marketing.

3. Job Descriptions

Most job descriptions usually tend to look very similar, so you need to make yours stand out. Most job boards allow you to see the first part of the job details before you actually go in to fully look at the vacancy. So, is your headline and the first section of the job description attention grabbing and would it make someone want to read more. Here's an example of one of our previous job descriptions that received a huge amount of inquiries.

LEVEL 3 Child Care Super Star Needed to Join our Awesome Pre School Team

✅ **Full Time Position**

📍 **Great Barr, Birmingham (B43,6NR)**

✅ **Excellent Salary with Monthly Bonus Potential**

If you're someone with a BIG personality 😄 that loves to dress up, paint, role play, sing, comfort, listen, support and care for each child as if they were your own V (very) I (individual) P(person), then you could be exactly what we're looking for 👁 👁 👁

BUT, If you don't think your special, then you probably shouldn't read on 😑 😑 🙄 🙄

You see, at Fairytales Nursery every one of our team is a Child Care Superstar in their own right and we treat them that way too 🤍 🤍

Here at Fairytales our Company Values are at the heart of everything we do. Afterall, you wouldn't want to work somewhere that had different values and beliefs than you, would you? 🫤

👪 Family - Means everything and we're all here to support each other.

😊 Communication - Is vital to delivering a quality service and the effectiveness of our team.

🙏 Contribution - To our team, our families and the local community.

🤍 Responsibility - To take ownership, lead when needed and be a positive role model for every child in our care.

😊 Customer Service - Always providing the best quality service to everyone including our team.

You'll notice that you can't even see the main job description on this page. It's all about who we are and what we believe in. If you'd like to get a copy of this template, go to www.childcaretoptips.com/resources

4. Company Benefits & incentive scale

Take a look at all the company benefits that other companies are offering. Be sure to list them all down and tick off which ones you offer. You'll probably find most companies are offering the same benefits. So, my challenge to you is, how can you raise your hand and stretch that bit further again? When I first started looking into our company benefits, I found out that both our insurance company and pension company offered a huge number of benefits for our employees if we renewed with them. Think about it, insurance companies and pension companies are all offering similar products, so they need to offer more to secure your business. Try reaching out to any of these companies or associations and see what benefits they have that you can promote to your team. Finally, are there any local businesses from your Dream 100 that could offer your team great discounts.

5. Your ideal candidate

I'd like you to take a look around your team and think about your best team members. What could you tell me about them? Do they work full-time or part-time? Are they highly qualified or extremely passionate, or even both? What attracted them to your business in the first place, and why have they stayed around? The next time you're looking to hire someone, I want you to think you're writing a marketing message to your best team members. What would you say, and what would be different to a normal job description?

The more you can pinpoint your ideal team member and talk directly to them, the more likely you are to find them. Of course, you can't discriminate against anyone, but if you know you're looking for someone that perhaps only wants to work part-time and isn't highly qualified in child care, but is extremely eager and willing to learn, include that in the job description. The problem is, that particular individual probably won't apply if you're just using a standard job description for a qualified teacher, as they won't think they're good enough for the role. Be as specific as you can.

6. Multiple platforms

Don't just rely on one platform. It's important to remember that not everyone is looking on traditional job websites. They may not actively be looking for a new job, but if you can encourage them with a great opportunity, you never know what could happen. So, you need to think about what platforms are people spending time on. Think about your ideal team member and where they'll be. Is it Instagram, or perhaps TikTok.

7. Build a sales funnel

This is another example of raising your hand and stretching that bit further. Don't just use job boards and posts on social media. Build a sales page (mini website) where you can direct people to find out more about your business. Have a video showcasing your business and lots of information about why they should come and work in your business. Give them plenty of ways to get in contact with you.

8. Use video

Video is a great way to show your personality and what your setting is all about. Creating a video about you and the business will allow people to connect with you that are attracted to your same values and ethos. We've had clients get their team involved in creating videos to showcase the culture they have in their business. After all, the last thing you want to do is employ someone that doesn't have those same values about child care as you. If you're a small family run business, it will help attract those that are put off by the large corporate facilities and naturally gravitate towards you.

9. Other ways to recruit

Here are some other examples of ways you can recruit:

Approach Colleges and Universities. They may have a child care course or similar running where students are looking for work.

Run free training days for staff from other child care providers. If you're already running a training day for your team, why not invite others along for free. It's a great way to showcase your business and your team culture. Even if they are not looking for a job themselves, they may then recommend someone else.

Incentivize your team and parents. They don't want agency staff, so they're just as eager as you to recruit the right candidate. So, why not incentivize them with perhaps a financial reward if they find you the perfect candidate.

10. The application process

Don't waste time on candidates that aren't a good fit.

That probably sounds harder than it is. One way to avoid wasting your time is to get candidates to go through steps before they get to you. Automate as much of the process as possible. If you've given them enough reasons to really want the job up until now, they'll do the steps.

Use video and text in your process

How many times have you sat through boring interviews. Perhaps you think someone looks good on paper, but when you meet them, they're not so great after all. So, why not get your candidates to submit video applications. All of our clients do this and it saves them a huge amount of time.

Use text to communicate

It may sound crazy to think you are text messaging someone about a job, but you'll get a way better response rate, as candidates can respond after work. People don't like picking up the phone these days, so we've managed up to 90% of the application process via text and it works great.

The interview process:

Getting candidates to show can be difficult. So, here are our top tips on getting them to show up.

Send a video of you and the team saying you can't wait to meet them.

Give them interview tips and preparation skills. They may be a great candidate, but they could just be really poor at interviews.

Send them photos of team gatherings to show how much fun you have

Give them a link to your calendar where they can pick a time that works for them.

The offer process:

Have you ever thought you've found a great candidate, only to call them and they've accepted a job elsewhere? Well, speed is key here.

Don't delay as good candidates go quickly

Follow up and get feedback quickly

Have your paperwork online ready to send quickly

The onboarding process:

This is the critical last step as to whether the candidate stays with you, so here are some top tips to follow:

Send them a welcome gift

Send them a personalized welcome video

Start pre onboarding them by sending them some content about you and the business

Onboard them gradually so they don't get overwhelmed

Shadow them and keep providing feedback

Set them up with a buggy system, so they have someone to show them the ropes.

Remember, applicants have the upper hand right now, so we need to market our staff vacancies just as much as we market our child care vacancies. Once you find a great candidate, don't wait around.

If you'd like to get a full breakdown of our Recruitment Model, go to www.child-carebusinessgrowth.com/resources

Onboarding A-Players

Lauren Lavington

I plan in this chapter to provide you with the assets to implement a fail proof onboarding process. Once you've mastered it, you'll be able to use it time and time again!

Getting the right steps in place is key to achieving greatness, and by this point you will have already established you can't possibly do it alone. We need to build a team of motivated and hard-working individuals who have the same goal in mind, and then empower them to be able to take the reins, so we can step out of the day to day and continue with the growth we are all aiming for.

So let's start at the very beginning of when a new team member joins you. You have probably onboarded someone before, to do something the way we want it done, seems easy right? You show them, and they do it, well it's not always as easy as it sounds - especially in child care!

Here are my top 10 tips on how to ensure your onboarding process works for you as an employer, as well as setting every employee up for success:

1. Make the new employee feel comfortable

We employ people because we want them to stay and grow with us as a business. I highly doubt anyone has recruited someone already thinking about having to replace them, so as with any new relationship, first impressions count. If you can make that person instantaneously feel comfortable within your company, they will be more open and receptive to learning, which is precisely what we need from them in their first few months with the company. Let's face it, all employers out there will say that they care for their team, but now we have to prove that we do. The whole world is recruiting right now, I'm sure it was hard enough to find someone you feel is right for the role in the first place, so now is about nurturing that relationship, and it starts on day one!

2. Plan your onboarding process out into days, weeks and months

Preparation is everything! You need to know exactly what is going to be taught and shown during your employee's onboarding and probation period. This will help both the parties know the expectations from each side. There's nothing worse than being lost in the dark. We all like to know the plan and where we are going. Having it mapped out will help you know where to start, but also show the employee what the end goal is.

Onboarding is not all on the employee, we have to work with them to help them become the team member we want them to be. Don't be a barrier to your on-boarding process, start today and map out what you think a new employee should be shown and when. Get a second opinion from a current employee or someone in a similar position to ensure you haven't missed anything and have the plan ready, before you even need it! You need to remove the excuse of an employee coming back and saying 'I was never shown how to do the task.'

(Top Tip: Do it now, get it out of your head and onto paper, then take a break and come back to it tomorrow. Share it with someone and then refresh it again. It's a process, so invest the time!)

3. Identify a person's strengths and where they need support.

People do not have weaknesses, identify the person's strengths and where there are development needs as early on as possible. Plenty of employers will interview and ask the applicant "what are your strengths and weaknesses" - we could probably all identify with that right? But would you liked to be asked to describe yourself negatively? I know I wouldn't - so always put a positive spin on what you say.

Everyone has something more to learn, so identify training needs - not weaknesses. Child care as an industry is so diverse; with the ever-growing types of curriculum, the types of child care available to parents and the difference between governing bodies and state laws, we can no longer assume that because someone is 'experienced', that they know what they are doing.

Teachers who are colleague or university graduates may know everything under the sun about children's development, but that doesn't mean they've ever changed a diaper or made a formula bottle of milk before, which is why we never assume someone knows what they are doing. You need to get an evaluation in as early as possible and tailor some of your onboarding plan to ensure it meets the needs of the individual too.

4. Assign a mentor or someone for them to shadow

Whether it be yourself or someone within the team that works how you'd like all employees to, having a role model makes the process easier as we aim for them to become a reflection of that person. Dependent on the position you are filling, you will no doubt have a wide range of different mediums in which the employee has to learn from, whether it be written assets for them to review such as, policies and procedures, or more physical on the job learning such as setting out activities and following routine.

Everyone learns best in different ways, so by giving them someone to observe will give them practical examples to follow as well as the written and spoken teaching they will receive too. 'One size' will never fit all, so we need to be as supportive and accommodating as we can.

5. Always round up what you're teaching

Don't let things drag over days and weeks. Everything we teach must be summarized and at a 'finished' point to allow them time to assess what they've learned. We're all guilty of trying to multitask and spin a variety of plates at the same time, don't let your bad habits hinder others. Make sure your teachings are well-rounded, tell them what you want to teach, show them an example, ask them to demonstrate back to you and summarize. There will be exceptions to the rule with some things having to be learned over longer time periods, but the aim should always be to accomplish something each day that they can feel confident in practice to do that they didn't know the day before.

You also should allow the new employee to be able to assess what they have learned the end of each day, giving them time to reflect on their progress and improve. Maybe even get them to keep a training log of their probation period for you both to review together - it's interesting to see if their log matches your plan of what you taught and when.

6. Encourage them and provide a safe space for them to ask questions

Everyone new will have a form of nerves coming in, new place, new people, new children, new policies - it's only natural to have a little nervous energy. We should aim to turn the nerves into positivity - we can do this be providing the supportive and safe place we spoke about at the beginning. Employees need to know that their questions are valid and that we are supporting them to achieve great things at every step. Telling them on day one, "if you have any questions, let me know" is sadly not enough. Remind them to ask if they need help, encourage them to voice if they understand or want something re explained. Provide a no judgement space for them by explaining 'we have all been there' 'no question is too silly.' Give examples to put them at ease and most importantly, handle their questions supportively, with well-informed answers!

7. Save time and automate what you can

I've said it before and from experience I bet you all know - recruitment is an ongoing process, something we have all done and will continue to do for as long as we are in business. So for those of you who've been in business now for a few years, I bet you've lost track of how many people you have onboarded. So, let's stop wasting our very valid time!! If you know you keep repeating the same things day in and day out when it comes to new employees - record it! Whether it's videos, screen shares, voice notes, written tutorials, getting it out of your head and into a solid training material will buy back some of that time lost. There are some fantastic software programs out there that can build you training areas for your team, such as www.childcareautomation.com where you can build a bank of onboarding videos covering everything from the story of your business, right through to how to fill in an accident form.

Be sure to get your team involved in creating the videos and distribute them to all existing team members, as well as all new staff onboarding. This will allow you to potentially even start onboarding from the day they accept the job. Infact, this is probably one of my most crucial points, as this will not only save your time, it will ensure all employees have the exact same experience during onboarding and also will allow them to refer back, recap and refresh on all the fundamentals of your business.

(Top Tip: make it fun and interactive - don't stress about professional filming, whip out your phone and just get it done!)

8. Don't wait until the end of the probation period to review their performance

Have you been there, where you've employed someone, first few weeks are going well.. something crops up and you take your eye off the ball and then bang! The probationary period is over and you have to quickly make a decision on if they secure their contract or not!

This is why you must have regular check ins - where you sit together and openly assess if the person is meeting the milestones you expect of them, address the training needs and action them. Don't let people slip through the cracks undetected! On their first day, block your diary bi-weekly or monthly, whichever you decide, for the rest of the probationary period. Once the dates are agreed, stick to them! This can link back to point 6, you are simply providing them with the safe space to ask questions and extend their learning. Remember, every employee is a direct reflection of you and your business.

9. Onboarding is only the beginning

It may sound sad, but it's true. You must maintain a high level of performance oversight with all team members by setting out your follow-up assessments, 1-1's or appraisals.

Ensure both you and the employee know the next steps. You are investing into this person, look back on all the preparation, work and time you have put into getting them to this point. Now is the time to continue a good level of support and guidance for the rest of their employment with us - we all know working in child care, no two days are the same, and we cannot predict what's around the corner. So, you need to be on top of development and training needs to keep consistent high achieving a-players in your team. Invest your passion into your team, ensure they are a reflection of you and your mission as a child care provider and I can guarantee you for as long as your values are aligned, and you are supporting them - they will stick with you.

10. Self Reflection

I've spoken a lot about the employer's role in onboarding, and how this directly affects the experience for the employee, but let's face it - we do get it wrong as an employer sometimes too. We are also always learning as our business grows and the industry changes, so make sure you set the time to review independently where the process went well and where there is room for improvement.

Your original plan for what onboarding will look like to a new recruit will undoubtedly change over time as the expectation on each role changes, or new roles are created, and it's all part of growth. So a key word for my chapter is evaluate, evaluate your process, evaluate the employee, and evaluate yourself - this way we are always on the right path to progress.

I hope you can get some key takeaways from this and implement them into your business. Take this as your sign to start today!

Lauren Lavington is the Operations Manager at Child Care Business Growth. If you'd like more information on staff onboarding, be sure to check out our website www.childcarebusinessgrowth.com

Having an Impact for Your Children

Vanessa Dooley

We are often too busy to focus on being in our business to even think about what we need to do to be 'ON' it. With the day to day running of our early years setting we get swept up by the dramas of every day that to even think about focusing on the next five years struggles to even begin to be words coming out of mouth never mind thoughts in our head.

So, with this in mind we have 10 tips to help you think about what you need to have in place to get the ball rolling. Remember Rome wasn't built in a day but take one step at a time and it will get you once step closer to your goal.

1. On the bus!

All the team need to be on the bus. Once on the bus the journey starts. This is the hardest part to be able to get the right people to be able hold onto your business and keep it going from one stop to another. If you do not have those people who want to be on that journey with you. Open the doors and gently let them off.

2. Speed of the leader, speed of the team

No team can lead itself and even though you were wanting to take a step back on being in your business, so you are able to work on it you still need to lead. You need to ensure you have a vision and the team are aware of that vision. Without you knowing your vision you do not know your speed and without that speed you cannot lead the team forward.

3. Reflection

Reflect on what you have done so far and record and celebrate. It will give you a sense of achievement and realise how far you have come. What is it that you need to do to improve? Whatever changes you need to make you need to have put those changes in place. Reflect on what you could have done better, think about your weakest area and what you are going to be doing to change it.

4. Protection

Ensure that all systems are in place to enable your team to work towards and go to when they are protecting children in the setting. Ensure training is kept up to date and this needs to be monitored. When cases of safeguarding and child protection arrive, which they will, ensure that the team are confident in how to respond so they feel confident and able to ensure that safety is paramount in your setting. This includes risk assessments and all other operational checks that need to be carried out monthly. Look at the organisation, the accountability, the team's knowledge, and the understanding of how vital safeguarding is. Do they know what safeguarding and child protection stands for and means in your setting? You need to get safeguarding right for the safety of the children, families, and the team.

5. Interaction

This is key! The team's interaction with children. Take a back seat and watch and see what your team are like when interacting with the children? Did they have conversations with their key children? Did they interact with each other? If they didn't, why didn't they? Get down to the children's level and ask open-ended questions, make eye contact. Bond with these children and have a good attachment to them. This is so important to get right and if your setting doesn't have these basics there is no point going forward. Every child learns from the interaction we give them.

6. Inspiration

Thinking about your intention each day, week and month– hopefully your staff team know that your intention comes from your last observation. This is where you see a child, you see what they know, and you extend it. They are going to use their interests to implement this. That intention throughout that day. Pinterest is great for inspiration for activities to implement but think about its impact. If it has no impact on a child's development in your setting, why are your staff team doing it? What's the purpose? You team must think about children's voices and choices and use that as part of their inspiration.

7. Progression

There are two pointers for this. One is for the children and how your team extend their learning, and the other is how are YOU progressing your team with training.

Are you recognising this in the supervisions and up-skilling their knowledge? What is it that you are doing as a leader or manager? What are you doing to up-skill? How do you progress where you need to be? What are you doing to take your setting to the next level? Are you extending all learning? Are you ambitious enough with your curriculum? That really is key.

8. Collaboration

It is what you are doing with parents and outside agencies to ensure you're working together to meet the children's learning and development needs. This is so important and something that may have slipped or taken a back seat over the past two years, so think about what you are doing currently and make improvements.

9. Be consistent

There is nothing like a leader who is not consistent

Your team need you to maintain what you are saying and preaching to ensure they are being consistent themselves. So, think about your core values and ensure they are being followed within your setting.

10 Learn by your mistakes

Every day is a learning day. Some days are good and some and not so great. But use those days to ensure you are learning. Take a breather and take each day as learning tool to help you progress to achieve your ultimate goal.

Jigsaw collaborates with you and your team to achieve the best outcomes for children. We are enthusiastic about ensuring you are promoting the excellent practice and that you can have a positive impact on children's lives. We deliver high-quality training and bespoke consultancy to all areas within early years, including childminders, pre-schools, and full day-care settings.

We are also able to supply a Quality Improvement Audits (QIAs) service which will enable you to be ready for your inspection and to shine throughout the process. This will be completed by an ex-Early Years Inspector with years of experience in managing Ofsted 'Outstanding' settings.

Vanessa Dooley the founder of Jigsaw is the Number 1 best selling author of Are you ready for your inspection which has helped hundreds of early years setting be confident in raising the quality in their setting.

We have an award winning accreditation which helps your team show the impact they are making and raise the quality of the setting

W: www.jigsawearlyyearsconsultancy.com

Guiding Your Team Through Conflict

Sindye Alexander

A Tale of Two Teachers

Laura is the lead teacher in the Butterfly Room at Tiny Tots Learning Center. Together with Kathy, her assistant teacher, they bring learning and fun to the three-year-olds of this mid-sized center. For the most part, the two work together like a well-oiled machine. They know the children well, they've planned activities, and can often anticipate each other's next moves. They often do kind things for each other, such as bring in morning coffee or treats, or swap classroom chores to help each other out. They seem to have a friendship that goes beyond just a typical "coworker" status.

That's why it was so unusual when Kimberly, an assistant in the two-year-old room, noticed that things seemed tense between them. She wondered what was going on but didn't want to get involved. Kimberly instead asked Dawn if she knew what was going on with Kathy and Laura. Of course, Dawn wasn't sure – but she *had a theory* that it had to do with extra work that needed to get done to prep for the next CLASS Assessment. *"Kathy obviously isn't pulling her weight and Laura is so stressed out."*

Unfortunately, this simple little question and assumption started the gossip chain and once it starts, it's almost impossible to reel it back. Kayla heard that Laura wouldn't switch a day off and Kathy was mad about that. Allison thought maybe Laura didn't like the way Kathy rearranged the Grocery Store Center and said something about it. And Janice speculated that Laura was not willing to do tasks that were "beneath her," expecting too much out of Kathy. *"That can wear on a person. No wonder Kathy's mad!"*

Within the hour, every staff member was sharing their theories with each other about what might be happening between the two normally friendly Butterfly Room teachers - all of them wrong.

There was obviously some sort of conflict, but without talking directly with the people involved, there was no way to know what the problem truly was or how to solve the issue. Openly speculating about the problem without the people directly involved only made it worse by spreading gossip and negative feelings.

Anna, the center director, knew she needed to get involved to keep this situation from festering and getting out of control. Anna was a strong leader and found ways to bridge the gap when her team needed help to keep the harmony going. Anna got coverage for the classroom and pulled the two ladies into her office to facilitate an open and honest discussion that would hopefully get to the bottom of the issue and resolve the conflict.

This chapter is dedicated to helping child care leaders that might not be as confident as Anna **to facilitate and communicate through workplace conflicts in a healthy way**, which is key to creating and maintaining a positive workplace culture.

The Complexity of Workplace Communication

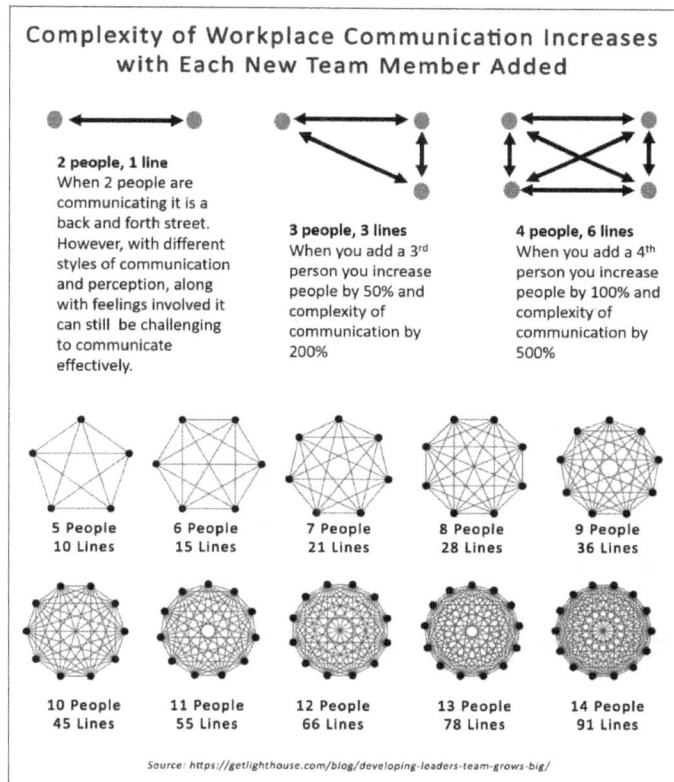

Complexity of Workplace Communication Increases with Each New Team Member Added

2 people, 1 line
When 2 people are communicating it is a back and forth street. However, with different styles of communication and perception, along with feelings involved it can still be challenging to communicate effectively.

3 people, 3 lines
When you add a 3rd person you increase people by 50% and complexity of communication by 200%

4 people, 6 lines
When you add a 4th person you increase people by 100% and complexity of communication by 500%

5 People 10 Lines | 6 People 15 Lines | 7 People 21 Lines | 8 People 28 Lines | 9 People 36 Lines

10 People 45 Lines | 11 People 55 Lines | 12 People 66 Lines | 13 People 78 Lines | 14 People 91 Lines

Source: https://getlighthouse.com/blog/developing-leaders-team-grows-big/

In a busy child care center, conflicts between staff members are inevitable. If your workplace culture tends to be more positive, you will likely run into fewer problematic conflicts. However, even in the most positive working environment, people can clash, causing some tension among the team.

Human relationships and communication patterns are complex, and this can lead to conflicts. Every time you add someone new to a relationship, you add a new level of complexity to the mix.

The diagram demonstrates how the level of complexity increases with each new person that is added.

Every person comes with their own experiences, thoughts, ideas, preferences, fears, and points of view. Blending communication between all of these different relationships and communication lines creates even more challenges to maintaining a harmonious workplace environment.

Conflict in the Workplace Can Strengthen Your Team

Conflict is a normal part of any relationship, and it can even be healthy. The fact is, it is absolutely impossible for two people to agree on every single thing at all times! Therefore, it is quite common for people with different goals and needs to butt heads from time to time. Luckily, this isn't necessarily a bad thing.

That's right! When handled positively and respectfully, conflict can allow coworkers to grow, ultimately strengthening the bond they share because they were able to get through a problem together and come out on top. It can also cause staff to develop a stronger mutual understanding and respect for each other, as well as build trust between the parties involved, and give them all a renewed confidence in their ability to work and solve problems together in the future.

Conflict in the workplace can also have a damaging effect. If it is not handled in a positive, timely manner, the underlying issues can fester. This will lead to a breakdown of teamwork, a personal dislike for each other, and eventual attrition. With staff turnover already high in our industry, it is important for directors to be as effective as possible at helping their team to resolve workplace conflicts.

Many times, the reasons two team members are having a conflict may seem trivial on the surface, but somehow, strong negative feelings were triggered leading to a workplace conflict.

These strong feelings tend to stem from an emotional need or insecurity in the workplace that isn't being met, or that is being threatened. Staff need to feel safe, secure, respected, and valued in order to best contribute to your team and be at optimal performance. When these basic needs of safety, security, respect, and value are in jeopardy, conflicts usually arise.

Seven Simple Steps to Work Through Team Conflict

It's always preferable that your team members are able to talk to each other and work through problems on their own, but sometimes they need help, and your intervention is needed. The next time you have an issue between staff members that needs your attention, try walking through the steps in this section.

The ability to communicate with your team and facilitate conflict resolution in a healthy way will be key to creating and maintaining a positive work culture. Please read through the steps below to better familiarize yourself with this process.

If you are nervous about leading members of your team to work through a conflict, feel free to read through this chapter beforehand to prep. You can even have the book open and refer to the steps while leading the meeting. Sometimes having the guidelines in front of you to refer to can help you stay on track.

Step 1 - Identify the Specific Issue

It is important that you and the parties involved actually know what the problem is. Sometimes people react to emotions or vibes, and just *feel* like someone is being mean or rude to them.

One trick to help you or a staff member truly identify the specific issue is to write it down. This helps you to reflect and clearly see if there is an actual issue that needs to be resolved, or if you are having an emotional over-reaction.

If a team member comes to you to help you solve a problem and isn't very clear about the cause, try having them write it down until they are clear on what issue needs to be solved.

Step 2 – Set a Meeting with the Involved Parties

First, be sure you know who is involved in the conflict. In order to find a resolution, all persons involved need to meet together in a safe environment, so they can be heard and become part of the solution. Leaving key people out makes it feel like a gossip session rather than a problem-solving meeting.

Once you've identified who needs to be involved, invite them to a meeting. Be sure to make it possible for all parties to attend by providing classroom coverage, choosing a convenient time, and providing a private place to talk (such as an empty classroom or office.)

Step 3 – Lead the Meeting by Setting the Tone

When you are acting as the moderator to help team members work through conflicts, it is your job to set the tone of the meeting. Open things up by talking through some simple boundaries and rules that you all agree on.

Keep the following in mind when setting the meeting tone:

- **Agree to the problem.** Chances are, the team members involved know that there is a problem, but because of different roles and interests, they are perceiving the problem very differently. (This is part of the complexity of communication that creates conflicts.) Make sure everyone is in agreement.

- **Agree that the goal is to resolve the issue** and preserve a positive working relationship. Remind everyone that the goal is not to prove that one person is right, and the other is wrong, it is to talk through the problem and come to a resolution, meeting the needs of the employees, while also preserving and maintaining your positive company culture. Having this understanding will allow the meeting to be much more productive and the effects to be longer-lasting.

- **All parties should listen with empathy.** Encourage participants to try to see things from the other person's point of view and put themselves in the other person's shoes to truly understand how the problem is affecting them. The moderator should allow time for both sides to clearly express their feelings. Remember, your role as a leader is more than merely to resolve a conflict, but to convey to your team members the feeling that they are respected and understood.

- **Protect each person's right to speak.** Enforce a "Listening Before Speaking" rule. It is very important that each person is allowed a chance to be heard before the other interjects, defending their own position. Things might be shared, causing the other party to change their perspective about the conflict. *Have you ever taken a softer position on a matter you were upset about after learning a bit more about the circumstances? It can happen.*

Step 4 – Openly Discuss

Allow your staff to openly and honestly share their perspectives about the problem, but before they start, remind them to try to follow these guidelines to keep the conversation positive and productive. Try to jump in only if things get heated, off-track, or to remind of the meeting "rules."

- **Remember non-verbal cues.** A calm tone of voice and a concerned facial expression can make a real difference when discussing a touchy topic.

- **Use "I" statements.** Telling someone honestly how you feel can be a very powerful form of communication. Talking about how you feel and what you observe feels less accusatory than saying "You." For example, try saying, *"I feel stressed when I have to remind you to help complete the jobs on our daily classroom clean-up checklists. I feel like I am nagging you, but I am not sure if you will jump in if I don't say something. I don't like feeling like a nag. I'd rather feel like a team or partners."* Rather than, *"You are lazy and never help with cleaning up unless I beg you to."*

- **Keep an open mind**. Sometimes it is necessary to look beyond the incident or perceived problem. Often, the individual perspectives of each person regarding the problem or situation are what causes the conflict, rather than the situation itself. *For example, Donna could have left her snack dishes on the kitchen counter "until later" when she'd have a chance to come back and take care of them. Kimberly could see this and assume Donna is lazy - leaving the dishes for someone else to wash. She then takes offense and complains to Nicole. Gossip starts and rumors flow, all because of a* <u>misperception</u> *of Donna's intentions with the snack dishes.* Also, keep in mind that when small problems are not addressed promptly, they can fester, causing them to feel bigger and more stressful for those involved.

Step 5 - Brainstorm and Decide on the Solution

Your team has had a chance to share their feelings about the problem, now it's time to come up with a solution. Begin brainstorming for solutions, encouraging everyone in the meeting to contribute ideas. No judgment. Brainstorming helps all parties to feel like they are a part of the solution.

- **Be open to exploring all options.** Write down as many ideas as you can. It doesn't matter if you think the ideas are good or bad. You will narrow them down, tossing out the duds as this discussion continues.

- **Move quickly through your ideas.** Don't spend too much time on development at this time. Just jot down what comes to mind.

- **Expand on each other's ideas.** Ask questions for clarity. Encourage input from everyone. Sometimes a solution is found by modifying another's idea.

- **Be creative.** Allow silly and out-of-the-box ideas to be shared without judgment. You never know what will inspire the actual solution.

- **Narrow it down to the best ideas for a solution.** Reading through your list of great ideas, it is probably clear which one(s) make the most sense. All parties probably also have a better understanding of each other's positions and what lead to the conflict in the first place. Discuss and decide on the best solution for your group's goals.

- **Confirm the agreed-upon solution**. Congratulations! You have successfully navigated your way through a workplace conflict. Write down your solution and make a plan!

Step 6 - Create an Action Plan

Depending on the complexity of your conflict, an action plan might be needed. It could be as simple as having a follow-up discussion in a couple of weeks to confirm that the bad feelings have been resolved, or it could involve several steps. Be sure to document your plan by listing all steps involved, who is responsible for each one, and the dates by which the action steps need to be completed. It may also be helpful to identify actions that should be put in place to prevent conflicts of this nature from arising in the future.

Step 7 – Follow Up and Track Progress.

This is often the most neglected step in the process. As a leader, it is extremely important that you follow up in a week or two to see how it is going. Add a reminder to your calendar if you need to. *Are the parties following through on their plan? Has the tension gotten any better? Has the problem been resolved?* Sometimes just a quick conversation in the hallway or teacher's lounge is enough. Just ask a simple question about how it's going and see whether scheduling a follow-up meeting is necessary. Most often, just going through this process is a positive enough experience to turn the situation around, and both parties are happy with the outcome. However, sometimes a secondary meeting is necessary. It is important that your team knows that you value them and their happiness on the job, so be sure to follow up!

When Conflict Resolution Does Not Work

As a child care LEADER, it should be your goal to cultivate a positive working environment. You should model professional communication styles and lead your team with inspiration to accomplish your vision. Part of that is facilitating conflict resolution meetings with the hopes that your team members can resolve their issues and get back to working toward the vision of the company.

However, sometimes no matter what you do, the conflict cannot be resolved. Sometimes you end up with a bad hire that was one person during her interview, and another on the job. Sometimes, despite their qualifications, you learn that your new hire is just not a "fit" with your company culture. Sometimes, a long-time employee becomes disgruntled or complacent, and there is absolutely nothing you can do to change it.

Whatever the reason, sometimes there comes a point where you realize that there is no fixing a situation. If that happens at your school, you may need to make the hard decision to let somebody go.

Keeping someone employed that is not a good fit for your center will do your business more harm than good. Your highly motivated and productive team members will become frustrated and disheartened having to deal with this energy-draining person day in and day out. Parents may also be turned off by this "square-peg" employee, but be reluctant to say anything. And the employee that isn't a good fit will remain miserable in a job in which she clearly does not belong.

As soon as you realize there is no coming back from whatever conflict you may be trying to resolve, start making plans to make a staffing change.

If you have enough flexibility with your current team, let the person go immediately. If letting this person go right away would make keeping your required ratios difficult, dig out your stash of previously submitted resumes or start advertising immediately. Make a plan for change and set that plan in motion. *Of course, be sure to follow any state laws or regulations in your termination process,* but don't keep someone on who is not a fit for the culture of your school. Prolonging the inevitable only prolongs the agony that you and the rest of your team feel.

**Parts of this chapter are similar to or direct excerpts from Sindye Alexander's book, *Relationship Roadmap: Real-World Strategies for Building a Positive, Collaborative Culture in Your Preschool.* To learn more or dive deeper into creating and maintaining a positive workplace culture, find it on Amazon.

****

Sindye Alexander

Sindye Alexander has over 25 years of experience in the child care field. She's owned and directed both in-home and commercial child care centers. After working with several business coaches, and with the help of her amazing team, she was able to grow her in-home child care to a small child care center licensed for 32 children, then move to a larger building expanding to 120 children. Sindye was able to fill her new school just three months after relocating due to her proactive marketing tactics.

Experiencing such massive results in growing her business caused Sindye to fall in love with marketing and the business side of child care. She sold her center in 2016 and joined the Child Care Success Company, where she served as the Director of Marketing and as a child care training coach for several years.

Sindye is especially passionate about inspiring child care leaders to create a positive workplace culture. Her book: *Relationship Roadmap: Real-World Strategies for Building a Positive, Collaborative Culture in Your Preschool* is dedicated to providing owners and directors with actionable tips and tactics for doing just that.

She now independently serves several private clients with content and digital marketing services, and is available to train or speak on topics related to workplace culture and marketing.

Sindye resides in northern Michigan with her husband, Chad. They have four grown children and three grandchildren. Sindye values time with her family and enjoys traveling - especially cruising! She loves helping other child care business owners and directors grow and succeed. To inquire about having Sindye speak at your upcoming workshop, conference, or other event: email: sindyealexander88@gmail.com. (You can also find her on Facebook and LinkedIn.)

Employer Branding

Beth Cannon

If you want to attract, train, and retain top talent for your school, you need a solid talent attraction strategy, and that is a clear, concise, reputable, and recognizable Employer Brand. Employer Branding is how you market your school to attract talent that is going to set up your school to be THE place to work with young children in your community. It's a direct reflection of your culture, core values, and vision. A strong Employer Brand will attract the right candidates, accelerate your hire rate, and reduce your attrition rate.

My unique window into the childcare space has shown me that there is great disparity among centers. It's not just the socio-economics and demographic data. It's *leadership engagement* that is a game-changer. In my experience, leaders who are intentional about their business AND their brand have lower burnout rates and greater job satisfaction because they don't haphazardly recruit, and therefore, they can intentionally retain the best people for their organization.

These 10 strategies will help you nail down your Employer Brand because your dream team is waiting for you!

1. Evaluate Your Current Employee Experience

Current employee satisfaction is one of the best benchmarks for evaluating a healthy employer brand. What would your best employee say it's like to work for you? Conducting an employee engagement survey is a valuable tool to know where you stand with your current staff. No news is not always good news.

By talking to your current team, you'll gain insight into what's working, what's not working, and how you can possibly make some low-cost tweaks to how you motivate and develop your team. You must talk to your team to find out how you can improve their employee experience, and keep your employees accountable for acting "on-brand" with your vision, values, and expectations.

2. Cultivate Your Culture

"Your culture is a combination of what you create, and what you allow." (Craig Groeschel Leadership) Most ECE leaders are experiencing post-pandemic PTSD, and we have allowed more toxic behaviors than we would have ever tolerated prior. A positive culture is not created in a vacuum OR without intention.

You want your new employees to know what it takes to thrive and succeed in your school. Intentionally casting a vision of what it looks and feels like joining your team will help your team work together to create the experience you expect them to deliver.

You MUST pay attention to the tension. It's equally important to know what's hurting your culture so you can focus your efforts on eliminating potential threats.

3. Review Your Reputation

When you assess your reputation in your community and in the industry, think in terms of how many people know about you, and what do they think of you, both as a place to provide care for children AND what it's like to work for you. The *Harvard Business Review* reports a bad reputation costs a company at least 10 percent more per hire. A few key metrics in assessing your brand awareness are to check social media, your website traffic, and reviews on platforms like Indeed and Glassdoor.

4. Reduce Your Recruiting Costs by Retaining the Right Employees

According to HubSpot, employer branding is critical to your bottom line. A good employer brand can reduce turnover rates by 28%, and cut your costs-per-hire by half. Additionally, 75% of active job seekers are likely to apply to a job if the employer actively manages its employer brand.

Managing your brand draws a straight line back to your culture...the combination of what you create and what you allow.

5. Rate Your Referrals

Are your current employees or families referring new hires to you? You want your team and your customers to be Brand Ambassadors for your centers. Leverage your employees to post testimonials, either written or on video. Ask them to take pictures at your next team-building event, then have them post on their social media with hashtags like #bestjobever #whyiworkhere #joinourteam.

Sharing content with your families builds trust AND gives them material to post on their own social media and share with their community. Use your parent engagement apps to post pictures for your families to share, and you just might find those referrals rolling in.

6. Consider Your Competition

You're no longer just competing for families, you're competing for job candidates. Chances are your ideal candidate is applying for multiple jobs. Will you win? Employees are researching companies, and your online presence matters to them.

Is your visual branding and messaging clear across ALL platforms? Whether or not you are paying attention to the story the internet tells about you, there is a narrative out there that tells who you are in comparison to your competition. Are you using high-quality pictures and videos to tell the story of what it's like to work for you and to be a part of a cohesive, supporting, and fun team?

7. Evaluate Your Potential Employee Experience

If you confuse, you lose. Are your job postings creative and clear? Is the application process streamlined and simple? Most ECE leaders I know are asking candidates to come in and fill out a paper application amidst the all-out chaos that's happening around them. Your goal is to quickly captivate the right candidates and connect with them for a discovery call.

Here are 3 simple steps to connect:

1.) Sift through the apps quickly and be aggressive about setting up the interview (you have to be clear on what kind of candidate will fit.)

2.) Respond ASAP via Text or Call (if you don't your competitor will catch them.

3.)Send a calendar link + set up a zoom interview (because you don't have time for a no-show)

8. Define Unique Differentiators

What differentiates you from the schools and your community is NOT just what curriculum you offer or how nice/not nice your facility is. You can take the information from your employee engagement survey and discover the great things that set you apart. Leverage the words and experiences of your current team to give potentials a behind-the-scenes look at what matters most to your school.

It's important to note that offering the highest hourly rate in your area might not be the ONLY thing that draws the best candidates. ECEs are heart-centered, passion-driven people who have a true desire to serve children and families. Feeling their work is meaningful and impactful may be more valuable than the biggest paycheck.

9. Overhaul Your Onboarding

Our industry is generally failing our new employees with outdated, ineffective practices that don't set them up for success at work. Here are 3 simple steps to audit your onboarding:

Pass on the paperwork. Do you have a simple way to digitally share forms without the time-sucking tasks of copying, organizing, then wait-wait-waiting to get it all back...which is extremely boring, incredibly inefficient, and results in duplicate efforts. When those forms are handed in, what happens? Yep - more work for you.

Insist on interactivity. Sticking an excited new employee at a desk to read through page after page of dry, boring materials can kill their momentum on day one. Use onboarding and training tools that include images and quizzes to increase interest on the part of the employee. Being able to self-direct their onboarding process can help employees get more from the process. There are so many FREE systems to streamline this process.

Toss the "textbooks." Stop expecting new hires to slog through manuals trying to identify what's truly pertinent to their job description. Being forced to "read and acknowledge" an employee handbook is a thankless task, and verifying they've done it is difficult. You don't just want your employees to go through the motions. You want them to be sponges, absorbing pertinent information – which means you need to make that information easy to absorb.

10. Create Clarity

C - Your CORE Idea - in one sentence, what is your brand all about?

L - LOVE Your School - what do you love to tell people about your school?

A - Who is your AUDIENCE? - what knowledge, skills, and talents are you wanting to attract?

R - RESEARCH Your Team - why do they stay; why do they leave?

I - Your IDEAS for your Team - how can you best motivate and develop them?

T - What is your TIMELINE? - how soon does it matter that you make positive changes to create lasting change?

Y - What is your WHY? - why is it important for you to be successful in running your brand and your business?

Beth Cannon is known for her unique and effective approach to equipping and empowering early education leaders and teams. A sought-after speaker, coach, and consultant, Beth is the creator of a variety of strategy development and training programs and has delivered thousands of transformational keynotes and workshops for conferences, retreats, and schools.

Beth has dual roles in the ECE world:

• A keynote speaker, trainer and coach for ECE professionals through Beth Cannon Speaks and Leader's Lounge Solutions, and a registered ECE trainer through several states.

• The owner of 12 Stretch-n-Grow franchises - an international children's motor development and enrichment provider that directly serves childcare centers - and has built the largest, most successful business in the history of the company. She's the author and creator of the Children's Fitness Instructor Certification Program, curriculum developer, and the Director of Corporate Training, having trained hundreds of business owners worldwide.

With a bachelor's degree in communications and education from the University of Texas at Arlington, Beth's certifications in business, fitness, and education cover her office wall three times over.

Website: https://bethcannonspeaks.com

FINANCE

Business Credit

Asia Rivers

Many of us recognize the importance of personal credit, especially when it comes to starting a childcare business. While it may be easy to assume that credit is something that improves itself by its own efforts and will quickly render profits, this mindset will only delay the inevitable - becoming burnt out!

You need to know how to build, protect, and utilize your business credit… If you are missing opportunities because you don't have the business credit to obtain funding, you don't know how to position your business credibility in the marketplace and you know your business isn't being seen as credible on paper, then this chapter will break down everything you need to know.

Here are the basics:

-Personal Credit & Business Credit work together to supply sufficient cash flow to the business.

-When personal credit is insufficient, the business cash flow becomes a slippery slope.

-Frequently, business credit is not enough to sustain the business operations or seize profitable business opportunities. The business may become cash flow broke, which results in business failure.

Failure to plan results in a plan that is likely to fail; therefore, start facing the obstacles ahead, and it will become a smooth process to maneuver around!

The childcare industry has several hurdles involving money: a high cost of entry, specialized equipment, low margins, and a significant business failure risk; however, if personal and business credit is built and optimized, the obstacle can transform into an opportunity with a maximum potential return on investment.

Let's examine the top 10 tips to establish Business Credibility.

1.) Plan for Personal Issues

The business directly reflects its owner, and the owner cannot pour from an empty cup. Take some time to map out external forces that may directly influence how what, and when you conduct business. Family comes first and is most likely at the heart of why you chose to start a childcare business. Ensure that there's a sound support system to handle family matters. It may not be an issue when starting the business, but once the business gains momentum, your time will be occupied on the business, but your heart will be worn on your sleeve. When family challenges arise, such as death, legal issues, divorce, and mental health breaks, you need a plan that won't drain your bank account due to reacting out of desperation or a quick fix to normal. A simple solution may be temporarily allocating responsibilities to another critical person or even creating a lean business model to lessen organizational spending due to lessened executive oversight.

2.) Restore Personal Credit

Personal credit will be the business's oxygen mask. When business credit is insufficiently established or fundability is shaky, the owner's credit will be used to resuscitate the business bank accounts. However, this is a temporary fix. Utilizing personal credit to cure long-term issues like decreasing profits will become a black hole. Racking up major business expenses using personal credit can negatively impact your credit score. Aim to build business credit instead. If there are personal credit issues, quickly obtain a copy of your credit bureau report. The fastest way to clean up the report is by utilizing a credit repair company. However, if you are limited on funds but have time to fix issues, then D.I.Y. it. Research credit dispute letters to validate debt and request removal from your report. Remember, the higher the score, the less risky you are to lenders.

3.) Establish the Business

Each state or country has its process when establishing an organization of the business. Most filings are referred to as "Articles of Organization." If you've managed to get established in business without being properly organized, make it official. You cannot obtain a business bank account or even a merchant account without this type of filing. This filing authenticates the business and secures your right to borrow money or conduct business using the business name.

4.) Apply for the Business Tax ID or E.I.N.

Apply for a Tax Identification number at www.irs.gov or by mail. Do not proceed without a Tax ID or E.I.N. Ensure that the business name and address listed on the Articles of Organization paperwork match the same business name and address on the Internal Revenue Service (I.R.S.) paperwork. Remember to store these vital documents in a safe place. Lenders or banks often require the business owner to supply this paperwork to open a business bank account or borrow money. In addition, if your state or country requires additional registration of tax accounts, such as a sales tax account, ensure to do this in the startup phase. Neglecting to do so may cost extra money due to penalties associated with unfiled returns.

5.) Apply for a Dun & Bradstreet Number

The Dun & Bradstreet D-U-N-S Number is a unique nine-digit identifier for businesses. A DUNS number identifies a company, similarly to a person's social security number; however, it's for a business. A D-U-N-S Number identifies a company's Dun & Bradstreet business credit file. When applying for a D-U-N-S Number, understand that there is a verification process to determine the rightful business owner. The information in your Dun & Bradstreet credit report comes from the Live Business Identity of your company, which gives them the insight to make informed decisions about whether a lender will lend money, resources, or references and under what terms. Note: It may take up to 30 days to be assigned a D-U-N-S number. DO NOT MISS THE VERIFICATION CALL.

6.) Open a Business Bank Account

When applying for a business bank account, usually, the business banker will ask for a copy of the Business TAX ID/EIN, a copy of your Articles of Organization filing, and your Driver's License/Identification. If the business contains partners, all parties must be present for signing documentation. Set up a business checking and savings account. Once established, focus on creating a proper business banking relationship. This relationship is beneficial for improving your communication with banks. The more you connect, the more they know about you and your business. Eventually, this connection translates into trust. Therefore, you feel secure while working on your business. In contrast, a business banker works to learn and understand your business goals, manage business portfolios, and help you learn to manage your business finances. Note: Research the bank's funds availability policy, operating hours, and availability of business products, such as business lines of credit and business credit cards before opening an account.

7.) Pay Business Expenses from the Business Bank Account

If you treat your business's money the same as your own, you risk your personal assets' exposure. The mixing of personal and business funds is called commingling. This means that you didn't keep up the necessary rules governing an L.L.C. or corporation that's a separate legal entity. The legal protection, often referred to as the corporate vale, is pierced, and the owner is legally responsible and may be responsible for additional tax. To avoid exposure, pay businesses expenses for the business

from the business bank account. If you can pay online, process payments as EFT/ACH Debit. You will need the business routing and account number to complete the transaction. Note: Make regular deposits into your account and limit the number of times and days that the account is overdrawn (N.S.F.). The lowest lending products are typically Merchant Cash Advances (M.C.A.'s), and the business must deposit at least $5,000 into the account monthly to be eligible for a loan. Also, remember that every business bank account has a bank score, like personal and business credit scores.

8.) Build Business Credit

Business credit shows lenders and suppliers whether a business can be trusted to manage money. Think of your business credit score to let others know whether working with you would be a high-risk investment. Those who apply for financing from lenders or who trade credit with vendors typically need a high credit score to proceed. The reason for this is simple. Your business credit score provides valuable insights into your company's financial history, from delinquent payments to bankruptcy (or lack thereof). Business credit is crucial to running a successful business—paving the way for a better financial future. Note: There is a tiered scale for business credit, and it must be constructed organically to maximize its leverage. Increasing the business credit score will result in several benefits such as personal credit protection, business financing obtained faster, and you'll receive better terms with suppliers.

9.) Ask for Credit Terms with Vendors

Asking for credit terms is simple – it increases business cash flow. By using a company's (vendor) product (or service) for 30 days without paying, the business is essentially getting interest-free financing from a company. For example, the HVAC unit goes out and needs to be replaced; however, you are in the middle of a payroll week. Instead of using the business revenue allocated for payroll, you now have 30 days to obtain the money for the repair while staying in operations because the HVAC unit has been fixed. It's a good deal if you can get it. And most large companies can offer, but the business owner must ask. Note: Typically, terms vary per the cost, the company, and the vendor's labor. These credit terms are often referred to as NET TERMS and are decided by the company or vendor owner. Make sure to read all small print because net terms are paid in full and not over time like a credit card.

10.) Hire and Retain Help

Keeping up with each step in the process may be overwhelming for a childcare owner. Remember, we wear multiple hats, and we can't be the answer to every problem. It stagnates our operational growth and leads to a bottleneck. Do not allow your business to be a bottleneck because you lack sufficient revenue to hire additional key persons to assist in the financial process. A step in the right direction would be to hire a Fractional C.F.O. A fractional C.F.O. will use their expertise to get down to the root of decreasing revenue, but also put together a solution to turn the operations around IF things take a turn for the worse. A fractional C.F.O. does more than produce Excel sheets and informs the C.E.O. about the bottom line. The Fractional C.F.O. answers those questions that lay somewhere between business and personal. The great part is that it's a business expense, and they are not on the payroll. Note: Meeting on a consistent monthly basis will reduce the risk of business failure; however, the C.E.O. must be accountable and coachable by putting systems in place and being honest.

Ultimately, being an owner means that you are the C.E.O. however you need a partner that understands the mission, values, and has the vision of growth through strategic financial steps to unlock the door for several financial opportunities. Get started today, and work to increase your personal and business credit score while taking the load off by acquiring a fractional C.F.O.

Most childcare owners lack the expertise and skill set to be their own Chief Financial Officer. You may not even be aware of what a C.F.O is or how they can help your childcare business.

A C.F.O. ultimately brings expertise to ideally grow your business through strategic financial guidance and uses a tool known as business credit, which is just as vital as personal credit.

If you'd like to find out more about Asia Rivers and the support she provides as a CFO, be sure to check out https://www.asialrivers.com

Child Care Tax Saving Tips

Nekea Whitson

As an owner of a childcare center, I know one of the most stressful times within the year is TAX TIME! When I heard the word "taxes" it used to make me cringe. This was up until I learned that taxes actually benefits business owners. If you hire the right tax expert and implement the right strategies into place within your business, you can save thousands in taxes. Today I will give you some tax strategies you can implement immediately that will save you thousands in taxes.

Let's break this down. Who is the tax code really meant to help?

You☐ That's right business owners, entrepreneur and/or investor, the tax code was created to benefit you. It was meant to benefit those who create jobs and unfortunately tax employees at a higher rate. The more money you make, the higher the tax bracket you are in. On average, an individual pays about 40% of their income on taxes throughout their lifetime.

Benjamin Franklin said it best "in this world nothing is certain except death and taxes."

Here's a list of ten tax saving tips ideal for childcare business owners.

1. Retirement account(s)

If you have not invested into a retirement account now is the best time to do so! Here are my two favorites ones, Traditional and Roth IRA. Roth IRA is an individual retirement account in which you contribute after-tax dollars. Your contributions and earnings grow tax-free. Roth is recommended for those who expect to be in the higher tax bracket in the future. With traditional IRA's you take advantage of the tax benefits instantly. This is best for individuals who expect to be in the same or lower tax bracket when retired. The max you can invest yearly is $6,000.

2. Hire your child

You can pay $12,950 to each child per year. The money you pay them is not taxable and you can also get a $12,950 tax deduction in your business (Double Tax Saving). A caveat is that you can also have your child put $6,500 in a Custodial Roth IRA. This will allow them to save money that will never be taxed in the future. I put my daughter on payroll when she was 7. She started to read to the children virtually online during COVID and now creates digital books and reads to our brainiacs virtually once a week.

3. Business structure

Your structure will determine which taxes your business has to pay and how to file. Many individuals have the misconception that you automatically save in taxes as an LLC, but that is incorrect! Both LLC and Sole proprietors are taxed the same meaning they both must pay income tax averaging (20%) as well as self-employment tax (15.3%). Totaling an average of 35% in taxes. You can avoid the self-employment tax by taking the S-Corp election. Many business owners elect this status once they have a net profit of about $50k.

4. Auto Expenses

If you use your personal car for at least 50% business use you can write off expenses related to your vehicle. This includes interest, insurance, repairs, oil changes, maintenance, tires and even these outrageous gas prices (use your business credit card to write off these expenses). Another auto tax tip is that you can write off 100% of a vehicle if it's solely used for your business. That is right, if you purchase a van used solely on the daycare that van can be 100% tax deductible.

5. Tax planning

Tax planning season is the last quarter of the year and December is crucial. You could prepay expenses in December for the following tax year if you plan ahead, which will save you thousands in taxes. Let's say it's the end of November and you realize your business will have a substantial net profit. Since you were organized, you know your numbers and come up with a game plan with your tax professional. At this point you can decide to purchase a vehicle or prepay expenses for the following year to help offset your tax liability.

6. Organizing business finances

Bookkeeping is crucial as a business owner. For effective tax planning you need your finances in order. Bookkeeping gives you a detail visual report and keeps you in compliant with the latest regulations. Setting up separate bank accounts can also assist you with organization. Open separate business accounts for income, expense, and taxes. This tactic will also assist with higher approval odds when seeking funding.

7. Food/Trips

Did you know you could have the IRS pay for your business meals and travel expenses? When traveling for business you can deduct airfare, meals, hotel, Airbnb, and car rentals. When deducting these items, documentation is key. For meals, keep a record of what was discussed, the amount paid, the location, and with who you were with. This is especially a great tax savings for spouses who are in business together; you can turn a date-night into a tax deduction, as long as you are discussing business and have it notated. When it comes to travel, you must notate the reason.

8. File and pay on time

As a business owner, knowing your tax filing deadlines(s) is vital. The filing due dates vary based on your business structure. If you cannot file on time and avoid penalties, you can file an extension (form 7004 for corporation/partnerships and 4868 for schedule C filers). This gives you a six-month extension to file your tax return. By requesting the extension, you avoid getting a late penalty of 4.5% per month of the tax owed and an additional 0.5% a month of late penalty of tax due. The max filing penalty can get as high as 22.5%. Keep in mind that although you are granted six months to file the taxes owed are due on the original tax deadline.

9. Home office deduction.

Many shy away from this deduction especially if they have a daycare center. Whether home based or center base if you have an office in your home that is exclusively used for business you are entitled to write off expenses that are associated with the portion of your home (such as utilities, insurance, and rent). The percentage of the cost that is deductible is based on the square footage of the office to the total area of the house.

10. Augusta Rule

With the Augusta Rule, homeowners can rent their home out for up to fourteen days, TAX-FREE. You do not have to report the rental income on your individual tax return. Keep in mind, if your home is your primary place of business, you cannot use the Augusta Rule. You can find out comparable homes through Airbnb.com. This will tell you the average price per day as well as square footage and rooms. Keep documentation of comparable homes including the dates. As a business owner you can take advantage of this by renting your home to your business. Let's not leave Uncle Sam a tip and use the tax code to our advantage.

Nekea is a childcare tax specialist that helps daycare owners increase their revenue by lowering their tax liabilities. She is the co-founder of Brainiac Enterprise, LLC and Brainiac Babies, LLC. Nekea decided to enroll in tax school several years back when she had her first tax bill of $10,000. Shortly after, she found out that if her business was just structured differently, she would have saved about $9,000 for that tax year. This taught Nekea that simple tax strategies are essential as a business owner, so she decided to assist her fellow childcare leaders in doing the same.

She partnered with Melissa, who has ten years of experience in the tax industry. Now, they both help childcare owners implement tax strategies and assist with funding opportunities to scale their businesses. They are proud to have helped hundreds of childcare owners during the pandemic to get approved for the PPP and EIDL loan. Nekea and Melissa continue to serve the childcare industry and keep them updated on the latest news through their YouTube and other social media platforms.

*** This is not legal advice as all tax situations are different. Please consult with your tax preparer or attorney. You can also contact me at 347-991-3401. Website- WWW.Brainiacenterprise.Com

Managing Finances for Growth

Ben McAdam

Managing your finances is not about painfully restricting your spending, or being buried in numbers or paperwork.

And the sole focus isn't lodging tax returns and other government compliance.

There are much bigger benefits in the whole "finance" area of your business than a lot of business owners are taught.

(In fairness, they are taught these things usually by the government or tax accountants, who naturally focus on the importance of record keeping and doing taxes properly, rather than how to grow your business.)

Managing your business finances for growth is about getting value from your numbers, in a way that won't take you much time, gives you an overview of how the business is doing, and helps you focus on the big priorities and big levers in your business.

Below are my top ten tips. At least one of them will stand out as something that you're not doing, or you feel you need to work on most, so implement that one first.

1. Get a bookkeeper, don't DIY (and try not to be too cheap)

There are more important skills to learn and things to spend your time on in the business than bookkeeping, e.g. growing revenue or hiring well.

Bookkeeper hourly rates can seem high when you first start your business, but remember that a good bookkeeper is many times faster than you, so paying for 3 hours is a great deal when it saves you 10 hours.

A cheap bookkeeper can take more time, make mistakes and require more input from you, so be careful being cheap.

If you find a cheap bookkeeper that's also good... intro me! They're super rare.

2. Reports should be designed to help you

If the reports don't make sense, or they don't help you understand what's happening in the business, then they can be changed. Use colours, graphs, more or less numbers, your own metrics... whatever is helpful for you (and whoever else reads them).

Your tax accountant will want reports in a certain format because of legal requirements, but you can have your own versions.

For example, one of the reports that I help my clients with bundles a whole bunch of small expenses into one row so that the many smaller amounts don't distract us from the important numbers.

3. Revenue goes up... ideally

The next few tips are about what the important numbers on your reports mean, and what to do about them, starting with revenue.

Ideally, revenue goes up over time, so unless there are seasonal fluctuations then declining or stagnant revenue is a sign that something needs to be fixed.

If revenue isn't going up, look at your marketing, sales and customer retention to try to find the leak.

And remember: don't mindlessly throw money at the problem, do small tests to find the right solution first.

4. Margins are the secret to your freedom and success

"Margins" simple definition: the gap between the price you charge and the cost for providing what the customer purchased (e.g. the workers who provide the service, not your marketing costs).

If that gap is small, then you'll hit a growth ceiling or work harder and earn less as your business grows.

With good margins, every additional customer provides more funds for marketing, growth projects, a management layer to free you from the day-to-day, more owner pay, and more profit.

To improve your margins, you could lower the cost side (through cheaper costs and/or productivity improvements)... or do the brave, but often necessary, option of raising your prices.

5. The Goldilocks Zone for marketing spend

In the story, Goldilocks finds things in the three bears' house that are too hot, too cold and finally something just right.

Your marketing spend is similar.

Too little spending means you'll have few potential customers to talk to and any sales conversations will be difficult, unless you've got strong referrals.

Too much spending is wasting money on bad returns, unless you're investing heavily (and wisely!) in growth.

The Goldilocks Zone varies based on industry, size, location and how fast you want to grow, but a good default is to spend 5-15% of revenue on marketing.

6. Pay yourself

Paying yourself is a careful balance, too.

Pay yourself enough to stay engaged in the business and not get distracted by personal money stress or by another source of income like a job.

But don't withdraw so much that you starve the business of the funds it needs for survival or growth.

Every 6 months, check you're not at either extreme.

If the business can't pay you a reasonable amount for the work you do, you can't hire someone else to do your tasks as the business grows, and it's also a sign that something isn't working in your business.

7. Reviewing the other expenses

Most other expenses are small or low impact, so don't obsess over them.

Every 2-3 months, run what I call a "Quick Profit Hunt" (google that and my website if you want the steps in a pretty PDF).

Basically, glance at every line on your bank/card statements for the last 1-3 months. For each line, choose to:

- Reduce it, e.g. decreasing the number of accounts on a piece of software
- Cut it, e.g. removing software you're not using
- Swap it, e.g. replacing software with a better/cheaper option
- Increase it, e.g. invest more in marketing that's working well
- Leave it, if none of the above apply.

It takes less than 20 minutes, and can find thousands per year in savings.

8. Measuring the non-financial numbers

Here I'm talking about things that don't appear on the usual financial reports, e.g. marketing metrics, sales metrics, team productivity, etc.

These topics have been covered elsewhere in the book, so my tip is to make sure you have systems or reminders to regularly measure the non-financial numbers, look at the reports, and decide what to do differently.

9. Ideal savings buffers

Be ready for negative surprises in your business (and personal finances too) by having a savings buffer set aside.

The ideal savings buffer is 3-6 months of expenses. If you're conservative, make it 6 months. If you're confident, make it 3 (or less).

Savings are also useful to take advantage of the random short-deadline opportunities that come up, like a competitor who suddenly wants to retire and is happy to accept less for their business if you can act fast.

10. "Can I afford to hire?" and other questions about the future

We can't *exactly* predict the future, but we can actually make *good enough* predictions for planning growth, new hires, and other big investments.

There are many software options out there, but the most useful is a spreadsheet.

Create a column for each month or week, for 3-6 months into the future.

Add rows of cash coming in/out, and a total down the bottom for how your bank balance changes.

Now you can run "what if" scenarios, like "can I afford to hire?" by adding extra payroll payments into the spreadsheet and seeing what happens to the bank balance in future.

Or you can experiment, risk-free, with how to grow faster without going broke.

Remember to update the projection with what actually happened, and learn to predict better by asking why your original prediction was different to what actually happened.

About the author:

Ben McAdam is a Profits Coach and entrepreneur. For over 15 years, he has helped hundreds of business owners all over the world grow their profits and gain clarity around their numbers, without judgement or confusing jargon.

He has an accounting degree, but isn't an accountant. He knows about tax and bookkeeping, but he doesn't do that. He's all about helping you use your numbers to make your business better and achieve your goals.

He wishes for you to have an enormous tax bill... because it means you've earned a lot of money!

More helpful tips can be found on his website and his podcast Business Numbers Podcast.

ProfitsCollective.com

Aligning Profit Goals with High-Quality Early Childhood Education Programs

Kathe Petchel

Make a Financial Mind shift

In business, the goal is to be profitable. Financial success is revered in many cultures and most national economies depend upon business success to grow. Without a thriving tax base, nations are vulnerable. Why then, do early childhood educators feel embarrassed or squeamish about being profitable? It's time to change the mindset of "it's all about the kids" to "in order to make it truly all about the kids, we must be financially secure." It's ok to make money! Our industry needs successful entrepreneurs to keep competition healthy, innovate and problem-solve and avoid the overstepping of government regulators. The more successful you are, the better you can support your family and the lifestyle you dream of.

Entering into the childcare industry is incredibly stressful, and the risks and liability owners assume when operating childcare centers should be considered carefully. On the other hand, the impact we make on children's lives and the contributions to our communities are impossible to measure. Without small business owners and their entrepreneurial wisdom and creativity, our communities and countries would be missing opportunities for growth, collaboration, and conversation. By being a strong voice for your small business, seizing opportunities for growth, and diligently guiding your team to excellent financial practices, your contribution to our world will be significant. You deserve to be successful.

1. The Basics: Know Industry Recommended Budget Percentages

Manage your budget using general industry best practices. At Hinge Advisors, we have over thirty years of financial data from both large and small child care organizations. We've analyzed the data and have general best-practice recommended percentages for each expense category. When working with clients, this benchmark is extremely helpful as a guide when budgeting and analyzing monthly P & L's, year-over-year progress, and growth plans. Certainly, regions of the country and particular situations will vary but knowing the best practice percentages that successful companies use is valuable information. Surprisingly, very few recommended percentages have changed over the years. One that has changed is marketing - social media is much less expensive than the old-fashioned yellow pages as well as print ads, and magazine and newspaper ads.

2. The Basics: Do Things Better (and faster)

In the book, The One Thing, Gary Keller recommends finding the one thing in your organization that makes you stronger and developing your skills around it. It's valuable to simplify each project or task to the one thing that is most important. Another key here is to be sure to delegate anything that is not in your area of strength or expertise. May I suggest one thing you consider is having strong financial systems in place? Consider these:

- Keep a tight rein on your books and your cash flow by reviewing weekly reports. Whether the platform you use automatically sends reports or you run them yourself, track your numbers weekly. Final P & L statements should be available to you within one week of the prior month's end. An essential report is one that tells you if customers are behind in payments.

- Sign all checks yourself and review all online payments ahead of time. If you auto-pay regularly for items such as rent payments, make sure you audit those accounts occasionally. The idea is that you know exactly what is going out.

- Regularly spot-check for system breakdowns. For example, most owners use Quickbooks or a similar bookkeeping platform that assists with financial accounting. Usually, it works well, but when my bank launched a brand new platform, due to a systems glitch, an entire month of credit card expenses wasn't downloaded to Quickbooks, resulting in some catch-up work. If you have third-party clients such as subsidy payees, keeping track of those systems is essential. If all paperwork isn't submitted correctly and on time, you risk the loss of payments. If your financial platform doesn't automatically charge for late pickup, late payments, or NSF checks, you risk losing tuition and other fees.

3. Listen to the experts

Dave Ramsey, a famous financial and business expert, advocates paying off credit cards each month, asking for lower interest rates regularly, and paying with cash whenever possible. Prices are going up for everyone and regularly checking your bills for accuracy and asking for explanations on any added charges makes a difference. So too does the habit of calling your vendors and asking for lower rates or negotiating longer and better rent terms. Dave also says that fear paralyzes your decision-making ability. There are few areas in business as feared as financial ruin, so take off the blinders and look at your books. Ask for help, there are plenty of generous and knowledgeable colleagues who will cheer for your success.

Kathy Ligon, Hinge Advisors President, is a strong advocate for early education owners having financial success through knowledge. As part of Hinge's client relations team, I spend a large part of my time researching and presenting education designed to help owners gain financial and operational knowledge. Kathy recommends that tuition rates be at the top or close to the top of your market and that they are raised a minimum of 5-8% at least once a year, more if you have neglected to raise rates or if you are not at or near the top of your market. If you have a true waitlist, raise rates for that age group immediately. Note that a true waitlist refers to a classroom with teachers hired and in place rather than a waitlist that will enroll once teachers are in place. Registration and re-registration fees should be charged without refunding and we do not recommend offering families vacation credit. In an effort to support hiring needs, we suggest that rather than offering as many family multiple child discounts, consider offering more generous child care discounts to your teachers.

4. Systemize and Automate

Make it as easy as possible for parents and third-party vendors to pay you, and for you to pay your team, vendors, and other obligations.

• Create and use a Financial Handbook or Manual-Your bookkeeper and anyone doing financial work should have a Financial Handbook or Manual to ensure each protocol is followed consistently.

• Automate payments for company bills using either online bill paying or via credit card but be sure to cancel when necessary or some automatically renew

- Automate collecting tuition as much as possible by having parents and third-party vendors set up online payments that will automatically be deposited into your account

- Use apps and platforms to stay in close communication with your stakeholders (parents, staff) and your potential families, and the greater community.

- Use your smartphone or an appropriate app to send yourself reminders of key dates each month so you aren't missing important financial deliverables.

- Automate deliveries such as food, milk, cleaning and paper supplies, classroom essentials, and snacks for teachers.

- Rather than spending time calling to set up regular essential work such as lawn care, fire inspections, HVAC, and other maintenance, set them up for the year. Negotiate a better rate for a yearly commitment.

5. Prioritize Profit: Look at your budget upside down

Stephen Covey, the author of The 7 Habits of Highly Effective People, hit the nail on the head with the concept of habits. One of my favorites is Habit 2: Begin with the End in Mind. Define clear measures of success and create a plan to achieve them. In the Book Profit First, Mike Michalowicz promotes taking disciplined steps to set aside a percentage of revenue as profit before paying bills. While uncomfortable, you will begin habits towards successful profitability.

• Start with the profit you want to make and plug in the expenses you can afford.

Pro Tip: A lofty goal to start with is 15%, assuming enrollment at 70%. As your enrollment grows, your profit will too. It's equally acceptable to start lower, as little as 1-5% will start the habits you need. Build from there, increasing the percentage as enrollment grows and you put other strategies in place.

- Take baby steps, by paying yourself first, and putting money aside until you have a minimum of 3 months of payroll and expenses. Some owners put this in a separate bank, minimizing the temptation to transfer quickly.

• In his book, Profit First, Michalowicz outlines specific steps including one of my favorites: The 10/25 Rule which suggests paying bills only in batches on those dates (10th and 25th) as well as transferring out designated amounts of money for your profit bucket.

• Interesting to all of our accountant friends is the flipping of the traditional profit formula. Michalowiczz takes issue with the old accounting formula, which says

Sales − Expenses = Profit

and instead rethinks it as:

Sales − Profit = Expenses

This method strongly advocates for an owner's success! Many owners have the notion that unless they are very experienced or already profitable, this can't work for them. It's much like an old-fashioned budget - you work with what you have, but you prioritize profit first.

6. Communicate Your Value

This is a good time to dust off your 'Why', a concept made popular through his book Start with Why, in 2009 by Simon Sinek. Knowing and living your why matters more as early educators than perhaps if we owned a dress shop. We serve young children who can't advocate for themselves and parents who may be fearful, feeling guilty about working, or under stress, we aren't aware of. Letting your school community know your vision and that your commitment to them means in part being an excellent steward of their tuition dollars goes a long way to build trust. And we rely on trust. Be sure to start with communicating to staff who have strong relationships with parents, and cascade your message outwardly from there.

Pro Tip- Don't be afraid to brag a little. If you're excited about something new you're adding, chances are they will be too.

7. Build Community Relationships and Resources

Can you hear opportunity knocking? Build relationships with several banks and have them consider you a VIP client. When there are issues, they will put your needs first. Use the relationships you build to quickly establish lines of credit, loans, and lowered credit card rates by maintaining good banking relationships. What other financial partners might you work with? Certainly resource and referral agencies, the SBA and your local United Way, Early Head Start, and state private owner associations, all of whom are wonderful resources. Always be looking for your next opportunity and seize the moment.

8. Work Your Way out of a Job

At Hinge Advisors, I speak with owners daily and many times they are considering their future exit plan or actively working towards listing their company currently. It's important that your company can operate well without you. You want to have a strong bench built so that if opportunity knocks in the form of an offer you can't refuse, you'll be well compensated but more important, your life's work will be cared for. I want you to confidently leave your company knowing it will grow and thrive from the foundation you set. Please reach out to me if I can assist you in this process!

9. Manage Labor Carefully

The highest expense in childcare by far is labor. Not only are we paying higher wages than ever before, but we are also faced with other financial challenges such as rising interest rates, soaring inflation, supply chain issues, and rising cost of goods. Be a good steward of your financial resources by considering the following strategies:

- Rather than giving raises across the board, consider tying higher wages to added responsibilities, expanded hours, or education goals.

- Schedule staff carefully and watch closely the first 30 minutes and the last 30 minutes each day.

- Overhire rather than overstaff. This means staffing appropriately according to ratios, your protocols, and philosophy, but many times staff are willing to adjust their schedules and will understand that overtime not only causes burnout and frustration but hurts the company's financial goals.

10. Consider Ways to Add Value to Your Business Now

Anytime you can increase your licensed capacity, it's a good day! Each licensed slot means revenue and gives you flexibility. Keep a close eye on the compliance regulations in your state and do not allow capacity reductions or changes without your presence and understanding. Ask for any allowable variances and grandfathered situations. Consider adding on to your facility if possible or looking at room uses. With many programs completely closed, agencies may be more flexible with capacity increases.

Another way to add value:

• Refresh and rebrand at least every 8- 10 years. Do you want to be ready to compete when bright and shiny moves in nearby? My wonderful friends at Better Beans Branding lead the way in executing this for the early childhood industry with innovation, forward-thinking, and customer care. I have learned so much from their team, led by the unforgettable Thad Joiner. Typical areas needing refreshing include painting, flooring, lighting, lobby entrance, signage, tour stop signs, and furniture, especially in public areas. To me having a beautiful environment for children and teachers to work and play in each day is priceless.

I am happy to answer questions about this chapter, strategize your exit strategy, or help with a valuation of your company in preparation for listing. As always, confidentiality is strictly maintained.

Kathe Petchel, Senior Client Relations

Kathe Petchel has worked in early childhood education since 1980. A graduate of Penn State University, Kathe earned her B.S. in Elementary Education with an early childhood emphasis. After teaching kindergarten and first grade in public schools, she opened her first child care center in 1984. She currently owns three locations serving more than 450 families in Charlottesville, Virginia.

In 2017, Kathe joined the team at HINGE Advisors initially as a staffing and operations consultant guiding clients through their transaction process. Currently, she is a Senior Client Relations team member, focusing on building relationships with potential sellers and working alongside colleagues including financial analysts and transaction advisors as a liaison to support sellers as they consider their exit plans.

A large part of the role is understanding the challenges owners and administrators face. Kathe is the content queen at HINGE creating and presenting on a wide range of childcare best practice topics ranging from hiring and onboarding, and day-to-day operations to financial strategies for growth. She regularly presents at state, national and international conferences and is active with a number of state owner associations. Recent groups welcoming Kathe as a speaker include PACCA, VCCA, GCCA, CQEL, Every Child California, Colorado ECA, McCormick Institute, AELL, NAEYC, and the World Forum on Early Care and Education

Hinge Advisors www.hingeadvisors.com and

Bright Beginnings www.brightbeginningsva.co

SCALE

How To Scale Your Childcare Business

Daphene Booker-Harris

Scaling your childcare business can provide the flexibility and freedom to live the life you've always wanted to live as you build your business enterprise. While early childhood education business ownership can be lucrative, it takes laser-focused clarity and hard work to be successful. Establishing your multi-location business in such a way that your company can maintain and grow even if you are not at the heart and center of every aspect of the day-to-day operations is paramount for the success of owning and operating multiple centers. Imagine the founders of McDonald's having to visit each franchise. That would be absurd! Could you imagine your child care center functioning like a well-oiled machine whether you are present or away on vacation, or attending a conference for professional development? Let me share with you 10 tips to help scale your center.

Owning your own childcare center is a huge undertaking that requires a unique combination of skill and expertise. While education and business savvy are important, people's businesses, especially children and their families, also requires patience and love. The need for quality childcare providers has never been greater. Even before COVID-19, families struggled to find quality childcare in their areas.

Create Long-Lasting Systems

Scaling your business for growth involves planning, creating lasting systems, hiring the right staff members, building processes and procedures, utilizing technology, and most importantly, nurturing relationships between you and the families you serve. Successful functionality of your childcare business is key to putting into operation simple and practical tools that pull together the best skills and talents of your team. It is important to empower team members by equipping them with practical tools. Creating structures within your organization will help to align your team as capable problem-solvers even when you are not present.

Removing yourself as the glue of your center, so that things will not fall apart while you are not there, will enable you to open multiple sites in a rapid amount of time. Your growth and expansion are as much relying upon your own personal development and care for your family as it is to create lasting systems.

10 ways to scale to multiple locations without being at the center of daily operations:

1. Have a Growth Mindset

Having a growth mindset is essential to the success of your childcare business. If the COVID pandemic hasn't revealed anything else, we have witnessed the impact the lack of childcare can have on a family, a community, and our society. Because of this unique position, as childcare providers, we have an opportunity to shine and grow our businesses to the highest levels of success.

What Is A Growth Mindset?

Having a growth mindset means that even in the face of challenges, adversity and phases of unknowing, there is still a deep belief that you can succeed and build your business and grow past any areas of challenge you may face presently.

A growth mindset is important because there will be times when you may not know what to do or how to do things, or you may face difficulties or challenges, but you must believe that your business can grow and develop, and it will. Through hard work and a winning attitude, you and your team become problem solvers during a time when parents are looking for solutions to their childcare needs. Having a growth mindset communicates confidence and calm to the people who see it. Believing in your business and the services you provide is essential for your business to grow to the next level.

Be Resourceful

A growth mindset views limitations and challenges as temporary and finds ways to access the tools and information necessary to achieve a successful goal. Learning to look past the problem to solutions is a fundamental building block of success. If you realize there is a particular skill set or area of expertise that you are not knowledgeable in, take the time to invest in professional development through attending conferences, hiring a coach, or seeking out mentoring from experienced more knowledgeable childcare owners.

Be Different

One of the highlights of my centers is the unique community events we host. Each year, the students, parents, and community members look forward to our one-of-a-kind, fun-filled events that show our love and appreciation for their support. These events have set us apart from other child care programs and helped grow our brand.

What sets your childcare program apart from others in your community, town, or state? Is there something unique about the décor in your center? Is your curriculum or teaching philosophy different from other centers that are merely babysitting services? Do you incorporate extracurricular activities like sports, cooking, art, or music? Are you or your preschool teachers highly experienced or educated? Are you open earlier than other childcare facilities in the area… or do you stay open later? Whatever your special sauce is, use it to your advantage by letting the world know that you bring something different and unique.

Adapt to your market

The old saying goes, "the only thing constant in life is change" and so we have to be able to adapt. The childcare industry is constantly evolving and growing. You can't simply rest on your laurels once you have had some success. You need to stay on top of your game and be vigilant in discovering the latest regulations and childcare trends. For example, 30 years ago, a daycare was merely a place where a child was kept safe and fed all day. That has changed significantly since the 1980s, however. Today's parents are looking for more than a babysitter. Parents are not the only ones looking for educational experiences for their children, but state standards are also raising the bar for preschool education. Parents also want teachers who are educated and experienced. They want rooms that are vibrant, colorful and full of learning and growth. Child care centers that do not adapt to change do not last long.

2. Clear Vision and Core Values

Including staff members in the creation of core values in your center is an important part of building a solid team. When your team members are part of creating the culture you want to see in your school, establishing core values, and building positive rapport, their investment is not just a transaction between you and them, but they can see that they are a part of something long-lasting.

What are the attributes you envision as key elements to the culture of your school? Do you want a fun, loving, family environment? Do you have a commitment to the highest quality standards in childcare? Are you committed to your center's brand as being at the forefront of the childcare industry? Are you focused on being up-to-date on state standards for your center?

Success does not just happen, it takes consistency and intentionality. Establishing systems that represent your brand and the core values of your business are important to the longevity of your business so that you are not the glue that keeps operations running smoothly. Developing a leadership team that can keep your center running even when you are not there is critical. Developing the right time begins with your onboarding processes. When inviting new team members to join your organization, it's important to have buy-in from current employees who can uphold the vision and core values you've established. Create a framework, mission and vision statement that others can quickly learn, understand and incorporate into the culture of your childcare organization.

3. Written Policy and Procedures

Policies and procedures are the guiding light of your childcare operation. Your policies are the systems you set in place that will guide the practices of students, parents, and staff members.

Within your policies and procedures, the following should be documented:

- Rules and regulations for how your business operates
- Parents Handbook
- Children's Handbook
- Staff Handbook
- Opening and closing times
- Fees
- Due dates for fees
- Outline everything about your program, arrival, departure policies

- Consent and permission from parents for recording, taking pictures, and written consent in order to post on social media, specifying which social media outlets you will be using.

The policy and procedures are a contract and should be explicitly written, making the expectations for all parties involved clearly written. There are a number of details to address in the development of your policies and procedures. Allowing yourself the time and space to think critically and research important issues to address when creating the policies you would like to operate by should be of high priority.

Handbooks are clear-cut tools for summarizing important information for parents and staff. The policies and procedures, on the other hand, are more in-depth documents that provide explicit policies.

4. Create a Functional Filing System

Maintaining the administration, planning and documentation of an early childcare center can be quite an overwhelming task. Having a systematic approach to organizing documents will help you easily access them when needed. The requirement to maintain records and important paperwork concerning the day-to-day operation of your center is one of the most important duties of your work. Filing systems are subjective to the user and can take on various organizational methods. Some centers might use a color-coded filing system, using a different color folder for each age group at the center. It is key to develop a system that supports your individual style and organizational preferences and the needs of your childcare center. Here are a few ways that I have been able to stay organized throughout my centers:

Know What You Need First

Having the knowledge of what is needed and when those items are needed is the first major component in maintaining your files. What are the important documents that you need to access on a daily, monthly, quarterly, or annual basis? Understanding what is needed and when can help you create a long term plan for how you fulfill requirements that are needed through a streamlined system. Ask for help from other childcare owners, your educational leader, or mentors for guidance.

Clearly Define Your Tasks

Are there documents that are needed daily, weekly, or monthly and what are the due dates for those documents? Being able to break down tasks and plan for when those tasks need to be completed can make your life much simpler.

Put Your Hands On It

Using binders has been a great way for us to easily and quickly access important documents without wasting a lot of time. Binders are also important methods for keeping all aspects of your program in an organized system. From finances and payroll to meals and transportation, your filing system will help you access information readily and maintain organization.

5. Childcare Software

Childcare software platforms can be an affordable way to manage your center. The day-to-day operations of your center can be streamlined through the use of childcare software systems. Often, the child-care business owner is faced with juggling multiple demands throughout the day. A reliable software platform will help to streamline many of the important tasks while making your life easier.

Management

Once you decide the platform that would work best for you and your center, you would be able to manage your childcare through web-based applications that can be used on any device. You would be able to monitor the child to staff ratios and be certain to remain in compliance and manage schedules. You would also be able to manage information regarding the children and families that are enrolled in your center as well as attendance and mail tracking when working with your food program. You can manage all aspects of information such as enrollment schedules, immunizations, allergies that children might have, and medications that they might take. You can be sure to have your finger on the pulse of what is taking place in each of the rooms within your facilities.

Parents can now be more involved in the day-to-day decision-making and better communicate with teachers and administrators when needs change using the latest technology.

If you can't afford your own website, create a free listing on a child care search website. Many child care search websites offer great resources , so you can begin to build a name for yourself on the internet. As your business grows and develops, invest in daycare marketing and create online marketing strategies for your center.

6. Electronic Payment System

There are dozens of software platforms that will allow you to automate the payment process for families at your centers. The days of accepting cash and maintaining accounting by hand are long gone. Having up-to-date payment structures will make your life less stressful and creates smooth and easy options for parents. It is guaranteed that your parents will appreciate any service you provide that will help simplify their lives, particularly parents with young children. Utilizing electronic payment systems is a win-win for both you and your families. Most consumers today are paying their bills electronically, so it would be a welcomed resource to also pay for childcare the same way.

A number of online platforms allow you to create profiles for families that will accept credit and debit card payments. The key is finding a well-established service that has a good reputation amongst child care providers who have entrusted financial transactions through that platform. Some owners use electronic bank transfers, while others use popular online platforms like Paypal, which can be connected to both credit and debit cards and or bank accounts. While parents could make payments that are directly from their banks or debit and credit cards, Paypal is often considered a safer option because it is a world-trusted transaction platform.

There are a number of advantages to utilizing electronic accounting systems for all financial processes. It saves you time as the business owner to focus your time and attention on other important things. The automated system cuts down on disagreements and misunderstandings between parents and yourself because your policies clearly state payments and fees. With an automated system, you don't have to worry about missing dates or times for important aspects of your business because it will happen automatically through the system you have set in place. Automated systems are a worthwhile investment, and usually, you will pay a monthly fee to maintain the system. The great benefit is that once it is set in place, you are freed up to do other things in your business.

7. Utilize Technology

Technology impacts every aspect of our lives today. Technology impacts the way we communicate, learn, and function in society. Our daily functioning and interactions predominately take place through technology. Not to mention, utilizing computers and Ipads for students' lessons is a cost-cutting alternative to paper, printing, and ink. Today's technology is evolving and there are a number of resources to choose from whether you are advertising, communicating with parents, or educating and assessing your students.

Advertisement

Today, in order for a business owner to remain relevant and maintain credibility, having a web presence is vital to the success of your child care center. Although good old fashioned word of mouth has been one of the oldest time tested forms of advertising, that is not the only way to let potential families know about the dynamic services you provide. Trusting that a satisfied parent will tell other potential parents about your site should not be your sole form of spreading the word about your services.

Why go tech:

- Communication with parents in one place
- Assess student's development and progress over the course of time they are in your center
- Teachers are able to manage and track students
- Assess the progress of students and staff members
- Can be accessed from anywhere
- Expansion and growth is much easier, as you'd only have to do it once when the system is created and then duplicate it for other locations

8. Email Automation

In order to maintain communication and build relationships with both your parents and team members, it's important to utilize automated systems. By using automated emails and text messages, maintaining communication and contact with parents is made simpler.

Childcare is a people business. Relationships are key to the success of your business. Each family is an important part of your bigger community. You must be careful with your relationships in this business. Although child care is very much a business, it's also something highly personal for families. These parents are entrusting you with their most prized and valuable possession – their child. You need to show appreciation of that fact and understand that they might want to be in constant communication with you. In many ways, their connection with you is their only connection with their child.

9. Onboarding Process

Ask any childcare owner, and they will tell you about the high turnover rate in early childhood education. Identifying quality early-childhood educators is one of the most important and often most difficult aspects of early childhood education. Keeping those educators over time is critically important, too. Along with keeping quality staff, educator training has also been determined as another critical issue in early childhood education. This is why the onboarding process in your center is so key and is important for the longevity of your center.

More and more childcare centers are offering professional development for new employees joining their childcare teams. Because the industry continues to grow and improve, it is important to identify the right fit for your center and provide training that will help them make a smooth transition into the culture of your center.

In my centers, new employees go through a 90-day probationary training process. Although most industry experts contend that it takes anywhere from 6 months to one year to fully assimilate a new employee to the culture and systems of your establishment.

First Things First

The first phase of the hiring process is checking all the boxes necessary to have an employee in your center. Focusing on the important legal documents, human resource policies and all compliance issues should be the top priority from day one of the hiring process.

The onboarding of new employees is a collaborative effort of current team leaders and staff members. During the 90-day probationary period, there is a clear blueprint and objective of the skills and knowledge the new team member

Setting Goals and Measuring Performance

Nick Williams

There's a very common business term, which states - what gets measured improves. Think about it, if you've ever tried to lose weight, you probably measure what you eat, or how many repetitions you do, and gradually over time you'll probably find that whatever metric you are tracking will improve. The same applies in business too. Maybe you're already tracking some things within the business, such as the number of complaints, or accidents in the setting. However, are you tracking the business performance.

In this chapter, we're going to take a look at why it's important to track these metrics, how to track them and how to ensure they are being reviewed on a regular basis, along with setting goals for the company to reach towards.

First, it's important to understand what does KPI stand for? It means a Key Performance Indicator. This can apply across all areas of the business, such as occupancy reports, or profit margins, or volume of inquiries.

Having KPIs in place are essential if you want to grow and scale your business. Think about it, how can you open multiple locations if you don't actually know exactly what it costs you to acquire a customer, or whether profits are increasing, or operational costs are too high. Every truly successful business has KPIs in place that get reviewed regularly.

1. Start to outline some KPIs for each area of your business.

Break it down into the 5 key areas of running your business.

Marketing   Sales   Operations   Delivery   Finance

List down as many things as possible that you'd like to measure / track. Then pick 3-5 KPIs for each area. Keep it simple to start, as you don't want to set yourself up to fail by trying to monitor too much. Remember, this is new and will create more work.

2. Look back over of the data

Look back over the data that you have for each of these KPIs from previous months / years and use these as a baseline to create a starting point of where your numbers should be. For example, look at your occupancy for each month over the last three years, month on month. Then, look at what the average occupancy has been for each month and use this as your baseline.

3. Realistic targets

Now you have your baseline, set a realistic target to improve these baselines over time. For example, if your current occupancy was 67% for September, set a realistic goal to improve this percentage for next September. Remember, some of these KPIs will be reliant upon other KPIs. If you want to increase your occupancy, you'll need to either increase your inquiry conversion rate, or increase your volume of inquiries.

4. Goals for your business

One of the most common factors amongst successful people is that they all have ambitious goals for their business that a tracked regularly. So, start by setting some realistic goals for your business that are SMART:

Specific: Make your goals specific and narrow for more effective planning.

Measurable: Define what evidence will prove you're making progress and reevaluate when necessary.

Attainable: Make sure you can reasonably accomplish your goal within a certain timeframe.

Relevant: Your goals should align with your values and long-term objectives.

Time-based: Set a realistic, ambitious end-date for task prioritization and motivation.

People overestimate what they can achieve in one year, but underestimate what they can achieve in five years. So, be realistic but optimistic for the long term plan.

5. What's your plan

Start by planning out what you want to achieve over the next five years and work backwards. Don't worry if you haven't planned that far ahead, just start with at least the next twelve months. Then, work backwards into quarterly goals. People often set yearly goals, but then don't review them for the next twelve months and get to the end of the year without making any progress towards their plan. By setting quarterly goals, it breaks up the yearly goals into more manageable chunks and gives you something far more realistic to aim towards.

6. Involve your team

Get your team involved in not only helping set the goals, but to own their part of the goals too. Your team will be far more invested if they helped shape the goals of where the business is going over the next twelve months. It will give them that sense of ownership and responsibility.

7. Share responsibility

Once they've help shape the quarterly goals, it's now time to pass out the responsibility for everyone to own their part in achieving those goals. For example, if you plan to have a much bigger presence on social media, this will be broken down into smaller goals. You may have one person responsible for creating videos, whilst another is responsible for uploading photos of the day-to-day activities on social media. Remember, these goals will also need clear targets to aim towards, such as five videos per week, or ten social posts. The great thing about breaking down these quarterly goals is that the responsibility is shared amongst the whole team.

8. Regular reviews

It's important to review your KPIs on a regular basis. Some KPIs may need to be reported on daily, such as attendance numbers, whereas others may be reporting on weekly, monthly or quarterly. You and your team decide the cadence of the KPI and in what format you want that information to be presented. Do you want it on a visual board, on email, or some type of spreadsheet, so it's easy to see performance over time.

9. Weekly meetings

We have a weekly meeting in our business called a Level 10 meeting. It is for all heads of departments to attend and bring forward their weekly reporting. The idea of the meeting is to give a quick overview of what has happened the previous week in each department and review the KPI reporting. Too many times business owners get distracted about every single thing that happens in the business in real time, and whilst there are some things you need to know about right away, the majority of 'things' can be shared in one concise meeting. Think about how much time this would save you. If you'd like to find out more about Level 10 meetings, be sure to check of the creator, Gino Wickman and the book Traction.

10. Level 10 meetings

These meetings are highly structured 90-minute meetings that have a particular format laid out below:

Check-in (5 min)

Always start with a win. Prioritize big company wins, but in slower weeks, they may include personal milestones of teammates, such as getting married, or an internal promotion.

Scorecard Review (5 min)

Report on the status of your top 3 to 5 metrics. Are they on track, or are there any issues? Focus on saying whether they are on track or not and mention the numbers. The idea isn't to give a long explanation here.

Rock Review (5 min)

Quarterly Goals or better known as 'Rocks' are the biggest and most valuable projects. This is where you say whether a project is on track or off track. Again, you don't go into the detail why.

Customer/Employee Headlines (5 min)

Share critical feedback from clients and employees. Try and structure the feedback in one sentence and identify whether it is good or bad. There's no need for further explanation here.

Action Item Reviews (5 min)

Now it's time to review the current task list. Which tasks are done? Do any keep getting postponed? Use this section of the meeting to discuss them briefly and identify the issues.

Issues: Identify/Discuss/Resolve (60 minutes)

After going everything to this point, you'll most likely have identified a few issues. Now is the time to discuss and resolve them. Before deciding on the solutions, make sure to prioritize the top 3 issues. You can't go through everything here. You'll also find that sometimes things that were highlighted as a concern from a previous week are no longer a concern and solved themselves naturally.

Conclusion (5 min)

End with a review of the updated to-do list and priorities for the week, and ensure there is accountability for all the actions.

Remember to keep updating the Level 10 meeting sheet throughout the week, as you don't want to forget any important points that you want to raise in the meeting.

If you'd like to get a copy of our Level 10 Meeting template, go to www.childcare-toptips.com/resources

The Level 10 meeting can take a while to get used to, but once you do get into the habit of having them weekly, it can be a big game changer for your business. You'll also find that you don't get 'bothered' throughout the week as much, as your senior team tend to keep it all for the Level 10 meeting instead.

Eventually, as the business grows, and you take on more locations, each head of department will end up having their own Level 10 meeting with their team, which will then be reported back to you at your Level 10 meeting.

10 + Steps To Finding Happiness As A Leader in Early Childhood

Vernon Mason Jr.

Why is it important to find happiness as a leader in early childhood??

Most people that begin working in early childhood are heart-centered. The characteristics that make you good at working with kids can often make your life supervising and leading adults difficult. It doesn't take long once we move into a leadership role that the responsibility begins taking a toll, and the weight of it all can make us react in ways that are not characteristic of us. I believe Simon Sinek was spot on with his belief, "Working hard for something we don't care about is called stress: Working hard for something we love is called passion." I do not believe we can love early childhood when its weight makes us unhappy. You cannot give what you are not; a stressed-out leader will have stressed-out staff. Then the question becomes how to find happiness, remain enthusiastic, charismatic, and lead in a manner authentic to our fun-loving personality.

My strategies for finding happiness and thriving rather than surviving as a leader in early childhood:

1. Not internalizing the stress of others

Once you become a leader, you quickly realize everyone wants to share their problems with you. Many leaders feel as if it is their job to have answers and be able to fix everyone's problems and therefore begin the dangerous habit of internalizing other people's stress. How do you listen to problems and not internalize or let them add to your stress? Your job is to listen to them; it is NOT your job to have a solution for their problem. So, listen to their problem to assure they feel heard, and your response should be a summary of what they just told you, not a solution.

2. Stop being the Fixer

Many directors and owners become the first person their team goes to fix all problems. We make the mistake of taking the challenge and giving our team the solutions, thus training them that we will handle all the problems. Then we get frustrated when we get phone calls at 5 am because someone has called in sick and the Leader in charge wants us to tell them how to cover the shift, or we take a day off, and the A/C breaks and they want to know who to call, or we're on vacation, and a parent gets mad, and they want to talk to you. We must train our leadership team to solve problems. Start simply with this response, "how do you think we should handle it?" Then each time they contact you with an issue that they should be able to handle, work them through their thought process and respond, see, you don't need me for this situation. If they make a bad choice, instead of reprimanding them, ask them, "what led you to that decision." And use the case in hand as a learning process.

3. Temporal Distancing

Temporal Distancing is also known as mental time travel. During stressful times, ask yourself, "will this matter in 5, 10, or 20 years? Think about where you will be and what amazing things you will be doing in years. This alleviates some of the immediate stress.

4. Setting Boundaries

My friend Chanie Wilschanski says, "The director who is always available isn't truly listening." I like to switch it up, get it into context, and say, "A director whose door is always "open" is not listening."

5. Realistic Expectations

What does a good day look like to you? No child gets hurt, no parent complains, no bus breaks down, the cook doesn't run short on milk, or no one quits. If any of these kinds of things happen and our day is deemed a "bad day," we will have very few good days.

6. Participatory Management

When you bring in the stakeholders and ask for input and opinions, you, therefore, are giving them influence over decisions that would directly affect them. We would all rather be asked for input rather than told what to do.

7. Taking the team concept from theory to practice

This is how an overworked leader, stressed out and headed for burnout, manages. Everything is dependent on them to provide the directions, the feedback, the answers, etc. Nothing moves forward without their input.

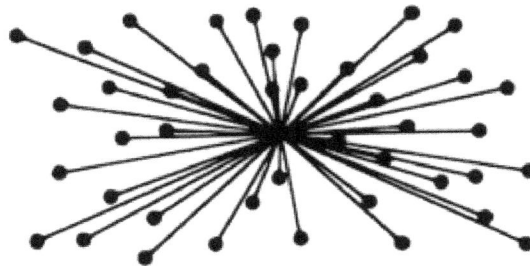

A Leader who engages a true team mentality in theory and practice sets up the environment, so most of what is happening are not dependent on their constant input and review. Training team members to make decisions and get input from others gives them ownership and develops buy-in.

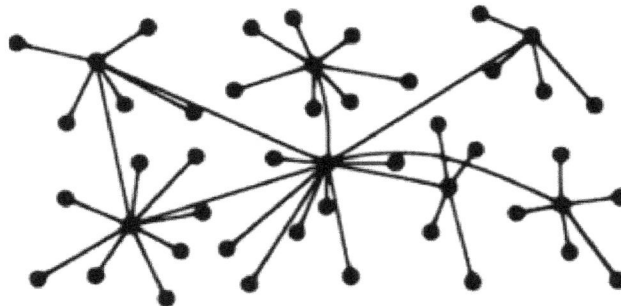

8. Finding the balance keeps you out of burnout

Self-Care, reward yourself. Leave the vow of poverty to the nuns. Pay yourself your value, take time off regularly, allowing yourself the time away to reignite your passion!

9. Becoming the employer of choice for the youngest generation

Our policies and procedures were written for Baby Boomers and Gen X generations. To become the employer of choice it is imperative to recruit Gen Z representation on your leadership team and not in a "figurehead" manner. Before changes are made, getting input from the Gen Z employees will lay the path for success.

10. Retention of leaders

Be the BEST Leader possible by leaving work at work! Stop the constant text threads all hours of the day and night. Allow your leaders to be off when they are off, DO NOT contact them on their off time! They must be able to reset, and the constant communication does not allow them to disconnect even if they are not physically there. This should also be done for you when you are off.

Bonus 1. Developing and showing empathy to our employees: Research shows that employees with an empathetic leader are more innovative, engaged, stay longer, and are more inclusive.

Bonus 2. Open financials: There seems to be a mystery around where the money goes in the early childhood field. It's so easy to walk into a classroom and count heads, multiply the tuition received for each child, and then assume that a lot of money is not being used in the program. The truth is it takes a lot of funding for early childhood programs to operate. We must move past this veil of secrecy and bring our leadership in to see where the money is used. Nothing will give a leadership team more buy-in than understanding the accurate financial picture.

Bonus 3. Remaining hopeful: New information and ideas brings hope. Reading, listening to a podcast, learning new concepts, expanding our knowledge base, or seeing things from a new perspective feeds our minds. This increased knowledge shows us that others are being successful, allowing us to remain hopeful!

Being a leader in early childhood is a big responsibility and touches many lives. We must prioritize our happiness to spread joy to those caring for the exceptional children we care for daily.

Vernon Mason has been an early childhood administrator for over 30 years with a master's degree in Early Childhood Administration from National Louis University. After rebuilding and starting over in just 2 years, Vernon grew WEE SCHOOL to 248 children. When he turned 40, he purchased 3 troubled childcare centers in only 12 months. In 2019 Vernon retired from operations of his five centers with 125 staff caring for 700 children. He is now Senior Vice President of Growth and Development for The Nest Schools and traveling the world, improving our community by spreading joy, advancing the operations of programs, strengthening the teachers, and the quality of care provided.

His keynotes have been described as "exactly what I needed" and "fall down funny." Some of his most requested keynotes and trainings are: Don't Waste a Crisis, where there's a will, there's a way, a story of perseverance in tough times; Avoiding Burnout by Finding and Keeping your Happiness; Tackling Turnover, praising and rewarding staff for little or no cost; Zero to Hero, improving an employee's performance or setting them free and Early Childhood/Preschool Classroom Management.

Don't Go! A practical guide for tackling employee turnover was published in 2015. Rhonda says, "Vernon writes with the humor of a professional who has battled in the trenches and come out winning. His openness and practical, real-life, "I've tried it, and it works!" will provide you with strategies to improve the culture of your organization and your skills as a leader.

Get Out! But before you go.....Practical steps to turn your Zero into a Hero or set them free! Published in 2018 is a guide for new and seasoned directors providing the steps and tools to help them supervise their employees, turnaround unwanted behavior, turn employees into valued team members, or to get them out—as I say, "Set them free."

Vernon is available to bring inspiring stories, humor, and content to conferences, corporate functions, and professional development events.

For more info: vernondirectorsleadership@gmail.com

When is the right time to grow your program?

Jessica Johnsen

When is the right time to grow your program or add more schools? Is it when your program is 100% full with a waiting list? When you have extra cash flow? When you love what you do and feel bored? When you see a need in a market? When you have perfected every single system and protocol? The answer is simple, all the above, or none of the above can be true. There is no "right time" or perfect equation. When you are passionate about what you do and want to serve MORE is when you should grow. Now that is not to say if you are bleeding cash, in a tremendous amount of debt, or drowning you should grow. Make good choices, but if you are doing at least ok, and you have a passion, GO FOR IT!

I like to say we are in opportunistic growth – there is just a tremendous amount of opportunity. Our company was not perfectly ready to grow. In fact, I was originally hired because the company grew too fast when they were not ready. However, in the short year after being hired, we were ready for more. Here are the ten steps that readied my company for growth, even when we were not cash heavy or 100% full.

1. Know your company vision.

If you do not know where you are going, you might end up somewhere else. Growth has always been a goal of mine. Personal growth, professional growth, and institutional growth included. That is how I set my vision. My ultimate goal is always to create a professional organization for people passionate about early childhood development and provide career growth opportunities. I genuinely believe that my company can positively change the future of our society and even our world. It is my responsibility to do that on a large scale.

I also encourage people to start with a 10-year plan and work backwards. How many schools do you want to have in 10 years? How many children do you want to serve? How many staff do you want to employ? What positions will you need? Lay out all these things on paper (easel paper is my personal favorite). Then do

5 years, 3 years, and 1 year. Do this exercise alone AND with your team. Do it at least annually. The goals CAN change, but hopefully because they get BIGGER. My team LOVES this exercise. They beg for it. Once everything is on paper, they put their names next to the positions they want to hold in each year.

2. Grow your team *early*.

Once you know what positions your current team members want to hold, start their personal and professional growth to meet those goals. What expectations go along with the positions they want? What systems, processes, policies need to be in place? What positions need to be hired? While it is phenomenal to grow from within, you will need a mix between inside and outside hires. You MUST never be the smartest person in the room, growth is not possible if you are the person who knows the most. Hire the people with skills you lack. You do not know what you do not know, but you must figure it out.

Egos aside, you and your team must be prepared to hire rockstars. Not every position can be hired from within. Have hard conversations. The higher the position, the MORE work, the LONGER hours, make this clear from the start. You never get promoted to less work or less responsibility. Make it clear, that a growth opportunity is also available within current positions. If your staff wants to be a rockstar in their current position, THAT is where freedom and efficiencies come into play. If you are growing and advancing, you are constantly putting in the work for that growth. Make conscious decisions and support your team to do so as well.

3. Find your funding model.

Whether this is SBA, financial institutions, or a blended purchasing model like I use, figure out what works best for your situation. My company was not in a financial position for traditional bank funding. BUT my team was in a position for investments and blended purchasing models. We have a group of investors who buy our buildings, and we buy the business. You can do this with investors, private equity, or a REIT (Real Estate Investment Trust). The most important aspect you show to these groups is a sustainable business model that is ready to scale. Find a broker you trust who understands cap rates and knows how to negotiate.

4. Have a plan.

You will NEVER feel completely ready for growth. What is the plan that works best for you? Talk with people who are where you want to be and who have done what you want to do. Personally, I do not like ground up builds. That is not to say I will never do one, but I am not passionate about designing buildings or classrooms. Nor am I enthusiastic about hiring a brand-new team of teachers to open a school, I prefer acquiring existing childcare centers. Even if the staff do not fit your culture (yet). Know what you want to do and then create a plan for it. Utilize your resources and honestly, utilize google. There is no reason to reinvent the wheel. STUDY ways other companies (even outside of our industry) have done what you want to do. Create your plan and share it with your team.

5. Execute your plan.

We have a process that works for us. We do a tremendous amount of due diligence which is a deep dive into enrollment, payroll, financials, turnover, and handbooks. We plan a SLOW transition from the existing brand to our brand. It's planned out in our project management tool, Basecamp. Every person on our team has their tasks to complete and a deadline. Our plan starts with Letter of Intent (LOI) and ends when the school is functioning without our day-to-day guidance. We know what each person does at each stage. We know how much work to put into each area of the plan. If a deal is not final, I do not waste man hours or resources preparing. The closer we are to closing date, the more energy and money we spend.

6. Expect the unexpected.

You will find skeletons. We have doubled our company each year in the past three years, and I have learned to expect the unexpected. There will always be delays, obstacles, and secrets about which we do not know. We expect these things, and they are not as traumatic as they could be. We prepare every person (including the seller) how to manage the unexpected. A calm person is a rational person is a trusted person. Be the calm person for your team. Set aside funding for HVACs and building repairs.

7. Assess your process often.

What is working for you? What is not working for you? Collect feedback from current and new staff. Sit down with your team after every step and add to your existing plan. My team takes extensive notes in our basecamp so that we can avoid and prevent mistakes. Even if you do not think you will grow anymore, you should always be evaluating your processes. It is easy to put an executed plan out of sight and out of mind but go back and evaluate what worked and opportunities for growth.

8. Makes necessary changes.

Whether they be process changes, or people changes, make the changes.... Quick. We are human beings. We make mistakes and learn new things. You must be open to change and be decisive. The best decision is the right decision, the second-best decision is the wrong decision, the worst decision is indecision. Publicly own your mistakes. Publicly celebrate your team and a job well done. Privately discuss other's mistakes and opportunities for growth, but do NOT ignore those mistakes and opportunities.

9. Keep going. Avoid the arrival fallacy.

There is no end game that you ride into the sunset if you are still in business. The end is retirement or sale. Period. If you are still in business, you've never "arrived." You must keep challenging your team and progressing. If you reach your goal of students, staff, or number of units, that is great, but the world is constantly changing. Your markets, demographics, and teams will constantly be changing. Keep repeating steps one through eight even if your vision changes trajectory.

10. Enjoy the PROCESS.

It sounds cliché, but it is true. The process IS your career. The growth, the change, the challenges, and the success are all part of the process. Just like children's art, the process is where the learning and pride occurs. You are not only building a company, but you are also building your own legacy. How do YOU want to leave the world? Your legacy is not created by the end, it is created by how you got there, the people you served, and the good you put into the world.

Jessica Johnsen

Jessica has an extensive background in the Early Education industry. She started in college as a teacher and eventually took over the Colorado State University Lab Preschool. Jessica consulted in the industry for over 5 years before moving to Washington DC and joining Georgetown Hill Early Schools. Jessica joined

Yellow Brick Road (YBR) in 2019 when the company was facing financial and cultural trouble. Jessica and her leadership team turned the culture of YBR around while navigating a global pandemic. They added their fifth school and second brand in November of 2020. Jessica and her team took on a third brand, Sonnet Montessori in June of 2021. The team then added their second market in Omaha, Nebraska, September 2021. Jessica expanded into her third market and added five more schools in summer of 2022. Jessica's team expects to have over twenty schools by the end of 2022. Jessica was nationally selected as a Top 20 Dynamic CEO's of 2021, featuring Jessica on the cover page. Jessica also held the cover story as a Beyond! Top 10 Powerhouse Businesswomen to Watch, December of 2021. Most recently, Jessica was named the 2022 CEO Of the Year – Education Sector for Business International.

CONGRATULATIONS!

You've come to the end of the book. We hope that you've found these top 10 strategies helpful for your business.

Please remember that each author / industry expert is expressing their own opinions and not the opinions of other authors within the book. Yes, you may even find some experts talk about the same or similar topic, but their advice will be different. That's totally fine. The book is here to give you that advice from multiple sources and allow you to make the right decision for you and your business.

If there is a topic you'd like to dig deeper on, be sure to reach out to the individual author through their contact details listed on their chapter.

www.ingramcontent.com/pod-product-compliance
Lightning Source LLC
Chambersburg PA
CBHW081240220326
41597CB00023BA/4226